JESUS IN THE BACKGROUND OF HISTORY

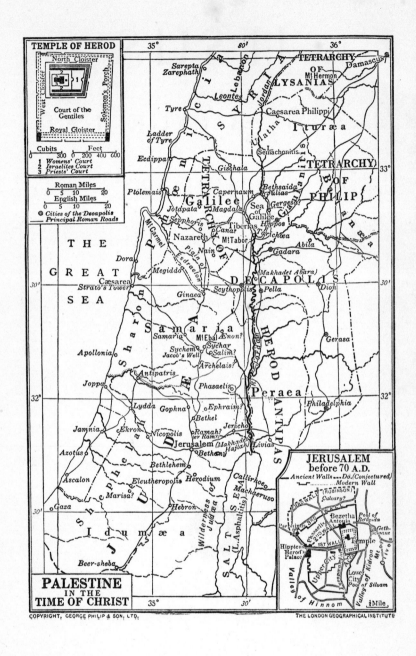

TEMPLE OF HEROD

North Cloister

Court of the
Gentiles

Royal Cloister

Cubits
0   300   Feet
0   200 400 600
1 Womens' Court
2 Israelites' Court
3 Priests' Court

Roman Miles
0   5   10   20
English Miles
0   5   10   20
◉ Cities of the Decapolis
Principal Roman Roads

THE
GREAT
SEA

Sarepta
Zarephath

Leontes

Tyre

Ladder
of Tyre

Ecdippa

Ptolemais

Jotdpata

Sephoris

Nazareth

Canar

Nain

Dora

Megiddo

Ginaea

Cæsarea
Strato's Tower

TETRARCHY OF

Mt Hermon

Damascus

TETRARCHY
OF
LYSANIAS

Caesarea Philippi

Ituræa

L.
Semachonitis

TETRARCHY
OF PHILIP

Capernaum
Bethsaida
Julias

Gischala

Magdala

Galilee
Sea
of
Galilee

Tiberias

Mt Tabor

Gergesa

Hippos

Dalchoa

Abila

Gadara

DECAPOLIS

Scythopolis

(Makhadet Abara)

Pella

Dion

Samaria

Sychem
Jacob's Well

Mt Ebal

Sychar
Salim?

Enon?

Archelais?

Gerasa

Apollonia

Antipatris

Joppa

Lydda

Gophna

Bethel

Ekron

Jamnia

Nicopolis

Azotus

Ascalon

Marisa?

Gaza

Phasaelis

Ephraim?

Ramah?
(er Ram?)

Jerusalem

Bethany

Bethlehem

Eleutheropolis

Herodium

Hebron

Idumæa

Beer-sheba

Jericho

(Makhade
Hajlah)

Livias

Peraea

Philadelphia

HEROD ANTIPAS

Callirhoe

Machaeruso

SALT SEA
(L. Asphaltitis)

PALESTINE
IN THE
TIME OF CHRIST

JERUSALEM
before 70 A.D.
Ancient Walls — — Do.(Conjectured)
Modern Wall

Calvary?

Pool of
Bethesda

Bezetha

Antonia

Geth-
semane

Hippicus
Herod's
Palace

Temple

Upper City

Mt.
of
Olives

Lower
City

Pool of
Siloam

Valley of Hinnom

Valley of Kidron

¼ Mile

JESUS

IN THE BACKGROUND

OF HISTORY

BY

A. I. POLACK

AND

W. W. SIMPSON

COHEN & WEST

30 PERCY STREET, LONDON WI

First published 1957

TO

B.H.P. and W.M.S.

Made and printed in England by
STAPLES PRINTERS LIMITED
at their Rochester, Kent, establishment

PREFACE

A MASTER at a Public School used occasionally to set his form as the subject of their weekly essay: 'Who is the greatest man who has ever lived?' Only once did he receive the answer 'Jesus Christ' – and that was from a boy of the Jewish faith.

This story, a true one, is not altogether surprising. The theological, transcendental conception of Jesus of Nazareth has tended to obscure his historical significance. He has thus come to be thought of primarily as the central figure of one of the world's great religions, and the study of his human personality and its impact on the purely historical process tends to be neglected. This, which would be serious enough in the case of the Christian believer, is little short of disastrous from the point of view of the large non-Christian world whose historical perspective has been seriously blurred by this failure to recognize the supreme achievement of one of the great makers of history.

This book represents an attempt to restore the balance and assess the permanent significance of Jesus' life and teaching apart from Christological claims. It is the joint product of a Christian who accepts these claims and a Jew who rejects them. Both are united in their veneration of the master-mind and share the conviction that its impact on all subsequent human development is, outside purely Christian circles, insufficiently appreciated.

Recognizing from the outset that in relation to some of the issues raised in this book there would be a fundamental divergence between us, we agreed that the original drafting of the text should be in the hands of the Jewish partner, and that his Christian colleague should play the part of critic and suggest emendations where he thought it necessary. Where no agreement was possible it was decided that he should explain by means of footnotes the reasons for his disagreement and what he believed to be the specifically Christian point of view. These notes will be found chiefly in the latter half of the book over the initials 'W.W.S.'

For some years we have worked together as colleagues in the specific sphere of Christian-Jewish relations. As a result of this experience we have come to believe that a better appreciation of the principles for which Jesus stood may contribute materially to the bringing more closely together of two groups of the human family who, for nearly two thousand years, have been separated by misunderstanding and deep-seated prejudice. It may also help to prompt a more active concern about those fundamental moral principles which constitute the common ground between Judaism and Christianity, indifference to which has led to the incredible things that have happened to Jews and Christians alike in our own day and generation.

This book was originally conceived as part of a larger whole, the first of two volumes, the second of which will attempt a similar assessment for the non-Jew of the nature and lasting significance of the post-Biblical development of Judaism. For Marcion has many followers even today who wonder whether it is really necessary for the Christian who has the New Testament to pay very much attention to the Old, and there are still more to whom it may come as an almost revolutionary suggestion that there is anything to be gained by a study of Rabbinic Judaism. But of that more anon. The second book has still to be written, and our immediate concern is with the first.

In the compilation of this book, we do not lay claim to any special scholarship or erudition. An assessment of the life and teaching of Jesus is necessarily a controversial business and cannot be altogether free from subjectivity. A great number of authorities have therefore been consulted but the authors are under a special obligation to the following who have worked in the same field: C. G. Montefiore, Israel Abrahams, T. R. Glover, J. Erskin Carpenter, C. E. Raven, Joseph Klausner, James Parkes, Solomon Zeitlin, H. E. Fosdick, Cecil Roth, E. W. Barnes, E. L. Allen, A. Cohen, Leslie Edgar, Norman Snaith, H. H. Rowley, and A. R. Stedman. Special thanks are also due to Mrs King-Lassman for so kindly looking through the proofs.

A.I.P.
W.W.S.

LONDON, *October* 1956.

CONTENTS

CHAPTER I

THE BIRTH OF A PEOPLE

'IF a biography is to be written the whole real truth must be told', wrote Tolstoi in his introduction to *Recollections*. But what is truth and where does the real truth about a man begin – and end?

Even in the case of a lesser man a biographer must start with some description of the environment into which he was born and trace from their source those external influences which have helped to shape his character and outlook. The great advances recently made in the study of psychology have shown that we cannot separate a man from the past experience of his people or the general trends of his age. This principle applies with a double force to those rare spirits whose impact on history may be described as epoch-making. In every case the 'something new' which they have added to human thought and development through their own native genius has some of its roots deeply laid in man's past experience. The teachings of Karl Marx, for example, can trace their descent through Hegelian philosophy to the *Republic* of Plato.

It will be seen then that the biography of an exceptional man may justifiably start at least a thousand years before his birth. This is especially true of Jesus of Nazareth, whose personality has impressed itself so decisively on all mankind's subsequent development. For he was a Hebrew of Hebrews and it is essential, if we are to understand the nature of his genius and his influence on man's thought and behaviour, that we should know something of the history of the people from whom he sprang.

Indeed, when we come to examine what Jesus said and did, his way of life, his outlook and the things for which he stood, we are constantly confronted with what psychologists call his frame of reference. No life is more closely related to events that happened a long time before than his. He assumed among his contemporaries and the audience he addressed an intimate knowledge of those events, and constantly quoted the actual words of men who had been dead for centuries. His teaching owed much to their original inspiration, while his whole theological conception was deeply rooted in the past experience of his people. The customs he observed, the hopes he entertained, the very terms he used – Law, prophets, parables, son of man, kingdom of God, to name only a few – are largely meaningless to us today apart from some knowledge of the sources from which they derived.

Still more does this apply to the exceedingly complex society into which Jesus was born. We shall find that his people were under the domination of a foreign power, the Empire of Rome, that his native land was divided into a number of provinces, and that the suzerainty of his own province, Galilee, was in the hands of an Idumean (Edomite) ruling prince. We shall read of the many factions into which the Jewish people were divided – Pharisees, Sadducees, Essenes, etc. – and of their diverse and often conflicting religious outlook. We shall discover that some of their chief institutions had Greek names – Synagogue, Sanhedrin – that their cosmology derived from Babylon, that the language spoken by the majority of the people was Aramaic.

Above all, when we examine the religious customs and ideas of Palestine in the first century A.D. we find a vast network of associations that go right back to the early life and story of the Jewish people. The commonplaces of religious vocabulary – Rabbis, phylacteries, 'unclean', Sabbath rest, eve of Passover, etc. – were charged with a deep emotional significance in the minds of the Jews of Jesus' time. Moreover, the Messianic hope that pervaded so much of the religious, as well as the political, thought of that period meant so many different things to different people that we cannot begin to understand it unless we know something of the circumstances which gave it birth.

The purpose of this book therefore is, first, to attempt a reconstruction of the historical background and, secondly, to indicate some of the ways in which a better knowledge of that background can help towards a deeper understanding of the life and teaching of Jesus.

The beginnings of the story are enveloped in the early mists that shroud all human origins. We read of groups of 'wandering Aramaeans' in the vast stretches of country that lie between the Euphrates and the Mediterranean seaboard, of shadowy patriarchal figures settling with their flocks in the 'fertile crescent', of long years of slavery under foreign domination ending in a great deliverance and the final achievement of independence and nation-hood on the soil of Palestine. All this is told in the familiar, picturesque language of the Bible. We should not expect to find there an accurate historical account of those early events, but we are fortunate in that centuries later, when the Hebrews became a settled people, there arose a group of teachers and writers who, for their own purposes, thought them worth recording. That these ancient legends are far from being pure myth has been largely established by modern archaeological research. To mention only one of many possible examples, Sir Leonard Woolley's excavations of the site of Ur of the Chaldees have disclosed a cultural back-ground entirely consistent with the Biblical story of the call of Abraham and his setting out in search of a 'promised land'. This might well have been somewhere about 2100 B.C.

In considering the influence of this ethnic background on the personality and outlook of Jesus we must obviously select some *terminus a quo*. The problem is to decide just which point to select. Nearly every people at some period or other becomes a prey to ancestral nostalgia and looks wistfully back to a distant past. They paint for themselves a picture of a golden or heroic age in which the old simple virtues flourished and man lived generously and free from corruption. The present seems to be squalid and vicious by comparison, and is often written or spoken of as an age of decadence. There is, as a rule, little truth in this artificial picture of moral deterioration. The march of civilization brings with it a deepening sense of purpose, a self-critical attitude and higher standards of conduct. It is simply that the few spirits who are first touched to fine issues tend to identify their inner promptings and aspirations with some glow of past experience in the dawn of their race's history. Sometimes a reformer deeply obsessed with the iniquities of the age in which he lives will deliberately appeal to his contemporaries in the name of one of the legendary founders of his race, hoping that through a literary fiction his words may carry an added solemnity and weight.

Such considerations are important in attempting to determine the period when the ideas which had a direct relation to the life and thought of Jesus first took shape. For some considerable time after their settlement in the 'promised land' the Hebrews were scattered about in small communities among the local Canaanite population. They formed, perhaps, a loose confederation of twelve tribes, whose spiritual centre was first at Shechem and later at Shiloh, where the Ark of the Covenant was housed. (An interesting parallel is furnished by the Amphictyonic Council in Greek history associated with Delphi.) The law of this Hebrew federation was the Book of the Covenant which it became the custom to read every seven years at the Festival of Tabernacles in the presence of a general assembly of the people (Deut. xxxi. 9–13). Somewhere about 1000 B.C. a monarchy was established in an attempt to repel the incursions of their neighbours, especially the Philistines, who had captured the Ark and destroyed Shiloh, and so had brought the earliest religious organism to an end.

The history of this monarchy does not in itself make particularly delectable reading. It is hardly distinguishable from others of its type. There is the usual succession of 'good' and 'bad' kings, of squalid court intrigues, popular insurrections, and dynastic exterminations. In 937 B.C. occurred the great disruption. The tiny state split into two yet tinier ones, Israel and Judah, which henceforth were generally at enmity with each other until in 722 B.C. Israel, the northern unit, was finally overwhelmed by the mighty Assyrian Empire.

THE PROPHETIC MOVEMENT

A distinctive feature of this period which gives it an important bearing on the life of Jesus was the constant tension between the nomadic and a more settled way of life represented by the monarchy and the established cultus and priestly hierarchy which were its inevitable accompaniment. The tension found its most characteristic expression in a succession of bold and independent-minded men whose opposition to the throne and to the 'establishment' was a constant source of embarrassment and a creative challenge to king and priest alike.

These were the prophets or *Nebi-im*, as they were called in Hebrew. This Hebrew term suggests some kind of connection with certain ancient guilds of worshippers whose rites were characterized by feverish dancing, trance and ecstasy. Their real function is much more accurately described by the Greek word 'prophet' which means, not a soothsayer or foreteller of the future, but a man who fearlessly utters or 'speaks forth' what is in his mind. It is because the Hebrew prophets were so vitally concerned with what they believed to be the will of God for their own day and generation that so much of what they had to say has remained relevant even to our own.

We shall return in a later chapter to a more detailed consideration of the way in which the emergence of this prophetic element in the Hebrew religion brings the early history of the Jewish people into relation with the personality of Jesus. Here we may note one or two instances of how they affected the political scene.

The establishment of the monarchy itself met with their immediate opposition. 'This great wickedness' was Samuel's judgment on the Israelites' desire to have a king of their own so that they might be as the nations around them. And the reason for this opposition? 'Because', declared the Prophet, 'you have God himself as your king.'[1] Again, David was behaving just like any contemporary monarch when he seduced Bathsheba and contrived that her husband should be killed in battle. No subject in any of the small surrounding kingdoms or the vast empires that succeeded them would have dared to remonstrate with his ruler for such behaviour. But Nathan was able to force King David into the position of pronouncing judgment on himself while the prophet left the palace unscathed and its possessor to the torments of his own troubled conscience.

Public policy was indeed always liable to come under prophetic condemnation in a way altogether out of keeping with the absolute monarchies of these distant days. They depended for their security on popular support or an uncritical mass servility. Both were lacking in the case of the Jewish monarchy. Nowhere is this more clearly demonstrated than on one of the rare occasions when Israel and Judah were acting together against a common foe, the kingdom of Syria (I Kings xxii). Ahab, the King of Israel, had enlisted the support of a number of 'false' prophets in favour of an expedition against Ramoth Gilead. But Jehoshaphat, the King of Judah, in spite of Ahab's almost pathetic protests, insisted on consulting another prophet, Micaiah, who was known to be 'in opposition'. When, after some prevarication, he opposed the expedition he was put in prison for his outspokenness. But the damage had been done, the seeds of uncertainty had been sown, and the expedition ended in disaster.

A great deal of early Jewish history is intelligible only in terms of this conflict. The northern kingdom and its capital, Samaria,

[1] Biblical quotations throughout are from the Revised Version.

fell in 722 B.C. and the bulk of the people were carried captive by the conquering power, the vast new Assyrian Empire, and disappeared from history. How much of this political failure was brought about by the constant denunciations of the Prophets: the fiery hermit, Elijah; Amos, who loved the simplicities of country life and hated the extortion and greed of the powerful; and Hosea, the tenderest of them all, who foretold the destruction of his people because they would not return God's freely given love? They constituted, indeed, a constant and formidable threat to the national state, as did that later Prophet who comes at the climax of our story. But like so many rebels against society, they have become a source of strength and encouragement to mankind in all succeeding generations.

The remarkable thing is that the same fate did not befall the southern kingdom of Judah. There were the same inherent weaknesses and the same potential threat to the monarchy in the shape of a prophetic movement championing the cause of the poor and downtrodden against the selfish aristocracy. The state was in fact conquered many times by foreign invaders, was frequently compelled to pay tribute and, after the overthrow of Jerusalem by Nebuchadnezzar in 586 B.C., suffered a series of mass deportations. Yet the people, whether at home or in captivity, survived as a distinctive group, as they have done indeed down to the present day.

THE DEUTERONOMIC CHALLENGE

No single cause can account for this phenomenon, but an event of outstanding importance occurred during the later period of the monarchy which may well have contributed materially to it. In II Kings xxii the story is told of the discovery in the Temple of a book which, when it was read in the presence of King Josiah, led to a complete reformation of the cultus. For this book, which is generally identified with Deuteronomy and is thought by many scholars to have been secretly written during the reign of Josiah's predecessor, Manasseh, who did his best to suppress the prophetic movement, was based upon the threefold principle of the centralization of religious worship in the Temple at Jerusalem, the suppression of all debased forms of the cultus, and an emphasis on the close connection between the ceremonial and the moral law. The king himself was not to be above the law but a servant of it.

The effect of the discovery of this book was twofold. In the religious sphere it brought about an alliance between prophet and priest (the significance of which must be considered in a later chapter). In the political, it meant the subordination of what today we should call 'state' to 'church'. For the first time a king, Josiah, proclaims his subservience to the moral law. The first 'emperor' has paid his homage at Canossa, and to be 'King of the Jews' no longer signifies merely despotic rights. We can summarize the importance of this event by saying that henceforth in men's minds the possession of secular power has generally carried with it some implication of divine ministry.

In the Palestinian scene the discovery of Deuteronomy produced a number of immediate and startling changes. There was a drastic suppression of local shrines and a purge of religious practices. The foundations of monogamy and a pure family life were laid. In the political field the change was altogether fundamental. The new alliance between king and prophet produced a unity and homogeneity of spirit in the people that ensured their subsequent survival. When in 586 B.C. Jerusalem itself fell before the onslaught of a far more powerful organism, the Babylonian Empire, an idea was already implanted firmly enough in the minds even of those who were carried off into exile to provide a basis for a distinctive religious way of life. Their loyalty to this idea may be compared with the passion for democracy which induced the Athenian army to set up their state at Samos in 411 B.C. after the triumph of the oligarchic revolution in Athens. Political or social conditions might change, but the idea was indestructible. It was the belief that God had called them to be 'an holy people' who were to be his witnesses before all nations of the world.

This new concept of a theocratic society was immediately confronted with what was to prove its severest test. Until this time there was no known instance of a people retaining its separate character and identity after deportation; the pressure of environment had always proved too strong. The inhabitants of the northern kingdom of Israel, deported by Assyria a few generations earlier, had disappeared. The same is true of many less significant states whose names have almost fallen into oblivion. But this did not happen in the case of the Jews. Scattered in small groups throughout the Babylonian Empire, they retained their separate social and cultural structure and looked with longing eyes to the day when the Lord should 'turn again the captivity of Zion'. This new theocratic conception of society received a further impetus from the teachings of three remarkable personalities, Jeremiah, Ezekiel and the unknown author of the later chapters of Isaiah, all in varying degrees showing the influence of Deuteronomy. Indeed, from a religious point of view their teachings had a direct effect not only on the career and outlook of Jesus himself five hundred years later, but also on the subsequent thought of mankind right up to the present day.

Of these three Jeremiah was perhaps the greatest political force. He had, like Ezekiel, foreseen the collapse of Judah and regarded it as a divine act of retribution. He boldly advised the people to resign themselves to exile, maintain their divine allegiance in captivity, and seek the welfare of the state to which they had been deported. Ezekiel, the priest-prophet and Deuteronomic disciple *par excellence*, drew up precise rules for the theocratic state which should be established after the Restoration. This restoration of the exiles to their land was still more precisely foreshadowed by the last of the three, whose name is unknown, but whose work has been included in the Bible in the Book of Isaiah. Through Deutero-Isaiah, as he has come to be called, the gift of 'prophecy' was developed to its highest level, and the influence on the whole of their lives of his insistence upon the idea of a divine vocation for his people cannot be overestimated. It was he who foretold the downfall of Babylon and the restoration of the exiles through the agency of Cyrus, whom he actually called the 'messenger of God'. But this was not to be the end of their trials. He (or one of his disciples) predicted that henceforth they were to become the 'suffering servant' of humanity and vicariously carry on their shoulders the sins of all mankind.

Both of his 'prophecies' came true, but here we are only concerned with the purely historical one. The downfall of Babylon took place in 538 B.C. Cyrus, its conqueror, started his career as a rebel Elamite prince. Partly by war, partly through fifth-column activity, he succeeded in making himself ruler of the neighbouring country of Media, and then successively overwhelmed Lydia and Armenia. It is told of Croesus, King of Lydia, that on consulting the Delphic Oracle he received the answer that if he crossed the River Halys he would destroy a mighty kingdom. Greek oracles throve on ambiguity; he destroyed his own.

The overthrow of Babylon is described dramatically in the book of Daniel. The last king, Nabonidus, was a scholar rather than a warrior and he placed the kingdom under the regency of his son Belshazzar. The capital was seized through treachery while the regent and his nobles were feasting. From the Jewish point of view this change of masters had far-reaching consequences. Cyrus, a Zoroastrian monotheist who worshipped Ahura Mazda, the 'God of Light', had little sympathy with the crude Babylonian polytheism or the policy of suppression towards other cults practised by the Babylonian kings. His sympathy was immediately aroused by the Jewish exiles and he issued a decree allowing them to return to Palestine. Forty thousand of them are said to have availed themselves of this great act of liberation and to have returned in their convoys to the land of their fathers. Those who remained helped them with gifts of money and the little state of Judah received a new lease of life which was to last for just over four centuries.

CHAPTER II

FROM CYRUS TO HEROD THE GREAT

THE period between Cyrus and Herod or, in terms of more intimate Jewish history, between the Restoration and the birth of Jesus, is sometimes regarded as an age of decadence and disillusion. It is true that the youthful buoyancy and national exuberance of the previous centuries are lacking, that the bright hopes of the pre-Exilic and Exile periods failed to materialize, that the people have become curiously introspective in their outlook and prematurely middle-aged. Yet, in the main, this judgment is a superficial one.

It was in fact a period of important social development for the Jewish people, of great literary activity and intellectual vigour. One is reminded of fourth-century Athens. Here, too, it is sometimes said that decadence had set in, that the fine flower of Hellenic genius had withered and the people had become self-conscious and uninspired. Yet this was the century of Plato, Aristotle and his pupil, Alexander the Great. So, too, the parallel period of Jewish history saw the foundations of Judaism firmly laid and the people fortified against the vicissitudes of fortune; moreover, there was born at the same time a new universalistic concept which was ultimately to sweep over the whole western world.

These developments were not entirely due to what took place in the little country of Judah, nor are they the products of Jewish genius alone. Henceforth foreign influence begins to play an increasing part in Jewish life and thought. It is not only, as before, a question of the impact on Jewish history of external events such as the victory of a foreign dynasty or the struggle between conflicting empires. Something more profound was happening. Through their close contact with foreign peoples the Jews began to be affected by their cultures, just as all subsequent Jewish development has owed something to the thought and ideas of the peoples amongst whom they have lived.

These five centuries can be divided into three periods: the

Persian (roughly 536 to 333 B.C.), the Greek (333 to 169 B.C.), and the Hasmonean, ending in the Roman conquest and the beginning of the Christian era. The divisions are to some extent arbitrary, but the mere fact that this choice of labels is a convenient one suggests some correspondence between the three nations mentioned and the developments which took place within the Jewish state.

The Persian period starts with the return of the exiles. No event of major importance, however, took place in Palestine until Darius I (522–486 B.C.) became master of the Persian Empire and completely revolutionized its system of administration. He abandoned the policy of ruling through native princes and divided his empire into twenty provinces called satrapies. These were administered by civil governors (satraps), but their powers were considerably curtailed and the danger of local insurrection averted by the appointment of independent military commanders responsible only to the throne.

This policy had immediate results on the little country of Palestine which formed part of the fifth satrapy of the Persian Empire, called Transpotamia, with Damascus as its capital. There had been sporadic attempts to set up some local administration at Jerusalem ever since the great deportations, and we read of a governor, Gedaliah, put to death through the conspiracy of a jealous rival who claimed descent from the house of David. After the return of the exiles there was a further attempt to 'restore the throne of David' and another descendant, Zerubbabel, was appointed governor with the backing of the two Restoration prophets, Haggai and Zechariah. His removal and possible execution were directly due to Darius's new policy of centralization. Henceforth from a political point of view no event of importance took place in Palestine until the reign of Artaxerxes I (464–424 B.C.), though the Temple, destroyed by Nebuchadnezzar, was rebuilt – a shadow of its former self, we read – somewhere about the year 516 B.C.

Fortunately Jewish life at this period was not confined to the Holy Land. The majority of the exiles had in all probability remained in Persia sharing the prosperous urban life of the general population. Nevertheless they still looked with nostalgic eyes to the land of their fathers and in particular to the focal point of their religious hopes, the Temple. News filtered through that all was not well in the little distressful country. The inhabitants were constantly molested by their neighbours and every attempt to secure protection was frustrated by hostile incursions. Finally a Jewish official in the Persian court, Nehemiah, obtained his master's permission to return to Palestine with the object of restoring some sense of security to his much harassed people. He returned in 445 B.C. and immediately set about rebuilding the ruined wall of Jerusalem, thus securing for the inhabitants a period of political stability. More important still was his policy of internal consolidation, which received a further impetus when Ezra, called 'the Scribe' – a term which combines the double meaning of lawyer and student of the Law (Torah) – returned to Jerusalem, probably in 393 B.C.

The mood in which the exiles returned to their native land was largely responsible for the revolution that followed. Among the many things which they brought with them from their long stay in Persia were a new alphabet, the Aramaic language, a new cosmology (Chaldaei was the Roman word for astrologers and the story of the creation in Genesis clearly derives from Babylonian sources), but above all a new exclusiveness. The leading and well-to-do families had been the first to be deported and had always regarded themselves as the true heirs of the Jewish tradition. Further, they had grown accustomed in Persia to a more civilized way of life and a permanent barrier grew up between them and the poor, unsophisticated remnants of the population that had remained continuously in Palestine. This was accentuated by the inter-marriage that had taken place between the latter and the Samaritans, a people of cosmopolitan stock largely imported by the Assyrian kings after the fall of the northern kingdom. Always sensitive on this issue and keenly aware, after centuries of prophetic denunciation, of the threat which it involved to their religion, the 'true' Jews treated these other elements as half-bred outcasts and apostates from pure Judaism. This policy, initiated by Nehemiah, was sealed by Ezra, who may be regarded as the founder of the Jewish religion in the sense of an established church. It had the salutary effect of safeguarding the purity of Jewish monotheism, but at the same time it created the new concept of a religious aristocracy from which were excluded all those who could not claim pure descent from the Chosen People. It was a policy which did not go uncriticized, for it was bound to lead to friction. We shall watch its effects through the Greek period which followed until eventually it was challenged by the revolutionary religious outlook of Jesus himself.

The weakness of the imperial autocracy during the days of Persian decline was shown in its failure to defeat the Greeks at Salamis and Plataea, in the constant insurrections of Egypt, above all in that large-scale raid so vividly described in Xenophon's *Anabasis*, when ten thousand Greeks successfully extricated themselves from the heart of the Persian Empire. A general revolt took place in Palestine in 351 B.C. and lasted for three years. At the end of it ten thousand Jews (according to the historian Josephus) were deported, some to Babylonia, some to a province on the south of the Caspian Sea called Hyrcania. No longer could the Jews be regarded as a nation in any purely geographical sense. Increasingly, as time went on, the majority lived outside Palestine, though their distinctiveness was retained partly by their attachment to the 'Holy Land' and the Temple – 'If I forget thee O Jerusalem, let my right hand forget her cunning' – and partly through their prayers and religious culture. In this they resembled the Greeks, the next people with whom they came into contact. Here, too, we must think of widely scattered communities living in the midst of foreign 'barbarian' peoples and loosely bound together by common ties of ancestry, language and culture.

THE GREEK IMPACT

Towards the end of the fourth century an event took place which gave a new shape to both Greek and Jewish history and ensured that these two peoples, so disparate in origin and outlook, should confront each other in terms of the liveliest intimacy. In 333 B.C., through his defeat of the Persian army at Issus, Alexander the Great became master of the whole Eastern world. This remarkable man, a Macedonian by birth but one who had sat at the feet of Aristotle and was deeply imbued with a love of all things Greek, had conceived the mighty project of turning the whole world into a vast 'city state'. This youthful fantasy nearly came true. By the age of thirty-two, armed at the military level with the Macedonian phalanx, at the spiritual with Hellenic cultural values, he had pushed his conquest right up to the River Indus and had overrun nearly all the kingdoms of the then known world, including both Persia and Egypt. His early death prevented any consolidation of this vast newly won territory, and the world became a kind of arena in which his generals – known as the Diadochoi – sought to carve out large slices for themselves. A confused period followed which ended in the Battle of Ipsus (301 B.C.) when Antigonus, the ruler of Asia Minor, was slain. This left two of Alexander's generals, Seleucus and Ptolemy, as the dominant actors in the Palestinian scene. One became ruler of Babylon and Syria, the other of Egypt, and the political history of the Jews for the next hundred years can be written in terms of the struggle between these two rival monarchs and their descendants.

Two internal developments in Jewish life during this period, also helped to mould the kind of society into which Jesus was born. The first was a change from theocracy to commonwealth. Ever since the publication of Deuteronomy and the alliance between 'church' and 'state' effected by Josiah the Jews had cherished the concept of a priestly ruler, the counterpart of Plato's philosopher-guardian, who should administer the state in accordance with ideas first formulated by the prophets. These had become crystallized partly through the teachings of Ezekiel during the captivity, partly through the practical statecraft of Ezra who first canonized the five Pentateuchal books and instituted Judaism as an established religion. The attempt to make Zerubbabel king had failed. Henceforth a descendant of the tribe of Levi (the traditional priestly clan) was substituted for a scion of the house of David as ruler in Israel. The High Priest assumed secular control as part of his responsibility, an arrangement which worked well enough at a time when there was little freedom of political action. It received its highest expression in the person of Simon the Just, who combined to an exceptional degree the qualities of religious leader and civil administrator.

After his death, the office became more and more involved in political controversy. Modern students of Roman history are sometimes surprised when they read that Julius Caesar, a man steeped in blood and political intrigue, should become Pontifex Maximus. But there is good precedent in Jewish history and the conception that religion should be independent of politics, though it finds some authority in early Jewish and Christian teaching, is a comparatively modern one. From the time of Onias II, who refused to pay his personal tribute to his Egyptian overlord, Ptolemy IV (221–203 B.C.), the high priesthood became a bone of contention between the rival families, the house of Onias and the house of

Tobias. This squalid conflict lasted until the office actually passed into the hands of an upstart, Menelaus, who did not belong to the high-priestly family at all. Such an outrage was intolerable to the Jewish people and was only rendered possible on account of their political impotence and the powerful support accorded to him by the Seleucid king, Antiochus IV, (175–163 B.C.) who at the time held virtual control over Palestine. These events, coupled with the policy now inaugurated by Antiochus, led to the suppression of the theocratic concept of government and the establishment after a revolt, largely religious in character, of a political common-wealth under the Hasmoneans (see p. 25).

Closely related to these political changes was the second internal development, which profoundly affected the character and outlook of the Jewish people during the three centuries before Jesus was born. This was the spread of Greek influence. In its purest form it had probably reached Palestine before the Alexandrine conquests and left its mark on the literature of the later Biblical period. Most scholars hold that three books in particular, Proverbs, Ecclesiastes and Job, were affected by current trends of Greek philosophy. But a much more tangible contact took place when Alexander and his successors overran Palestine and the adjacent countries. Not only did Jews penetrate through infiltration or deportation into the cities of the newly Hellenized world such as Alexandria, but invading princes and armies brought Greek habits and modes of life into the very centres of Hebrism. Thus for the first time in their history the Jewish people, whose whole outlook rested on conceptions of simplicity, purity and holiness, were challenged by an intellectual, aesthetic and highly cultivated form of paganism.

It must not be thought that the new influence was entirely evil. Primitive simplicity often wears a halo in the minds of those who belong to more complex civilizations, but it narrows the horizon and may confront the lure and adventure of life in its fullness with a bleak denial. The Jews, more than most ancient peoples, were liable to 'wrap themselves up in their own virtue' and had tended, particularly since the separatist movement of Ezra and the sub-sequent drawing of 'a fence around the law', to live mentally in an ivory tower. They concentrated on a study of their own past history and looked with suspicion on all foreign cultures. This attitude was undeniably a source of strength, but it could be carried to dangerous limits. Fortunately the advent of the Greeks

shook their complacency and they were never afterwards able to
retire entirely into their own shell. Its benefits can be seen in the
Greek translation of the Bible, the Septuagint – necessitated by
the Alexandrine Jews' ignorance of Hebrew – in the Apocryphal
writings, and in the works of Philo and Josephus in the first
century A.D. Moreover, had it not been for Greek influence the
epoch-making epistles of the Hellenized Jew, Paul of Tarsus,
would never have been written in their present form.

But it was not the pure ray of Hellenic thought that swept over
Palestine in the wake of Alexander's armies and those of his
successors. When Juvenal complained that Imperial Rome had
become a 'Greek city' he used a revealing phrase: *in Tiberim
defluxit Orontes*, 'the Orontes has flowed into the Tiber'. The
Orontes is a Syrian river, and the arch-declaimer is bemoaning the
fact that the dregs of the East are defiling the pure Roman stream.
Hellenistic culture contained, indeed, but a thin veneer of Hellen-
ism superimposed on existing Oriental ways of life. As sometimes
happens in the case of such hybrids, the worst of both types was
retained, the best discarded. We are not, therefore, to think of the
Greece of Aeschylus or the Parthenon or the Funeral Speech of
Pericles; we must picture a blend of Oriental magnificence,
ruthlessness and lust for power with the sensual and often licen-
tious cult associated with the gymnasium and the temples of the
Olympian deities.

In spite of their background of Torah and pure monotheism
many Jews, particularly of the wealthier and ruling classes, fell an
easy prey to these allurements. It became the fashion to admire
anything Greek, their architecture, their clothing, even their
names. Priests actually left their Temple duties in order to take
part in Greek athletics. The purity of the Hebrew way of life was
seriously threatened.

How far this process would have gone will never be known, for
an event occurred which produced a most powerful reaction and
led to a violent reassertion of Hebraic values. We have seen how
the Seleucid king, Antiochus IV (who called himself Epiphanes,
'the illustrious'), had supported the non-Levitical Menelaus in the
high priesthood. In 169 B.C. it was falsely rumoured that he had
been killed while fighting in Egypt. Immediately the priestly party
drove Menelaus out of Jerusalem and appointed Jason, a member
of the Oniad family, in his place. This act of insubordination

determined Antiochus, on his return, to suppress the turbulent Jewish nation and stamp out their religion. A further motive for this reckless and cruel policy was the growing menace of Rome, which made the consolidation of his own empire necessary as a measure of self-defence.

THE HASMONEANS

Antiochus had to learn the hard lesson that the attempt to produce cultural uniformity in a state eventually defeats its own objects. After a short, pathetic period of non-resistance when the Jews were compelled to eat swine's flesh, to offer sacrifice to heathen deities, to witness the erection of an altar to Olympian Zeus in the Temple itself, they burst into open revolt under the leadership of an aged priest, Mattathias, and his five sons, known as the Maccabees. After a fluctuating struggle which lasted for many years the rebels succeeded in defeating the vastly superior forces of their Syrian oppressors, and Judas, the third and greatest of the brothers, was able to reconsecrate the Temple and restore religious independence. For a short time, too, the Jewish people became a secular power to be reckoned with. They had proved themselves in battle and gradually, in place of the theocratic, politically dependent state, there was established a strong, formidable and autonomous commonwealth.

The climax of this development was reached under the leadership of three ruling members of the Hasmonean dynasty, Simon, the last of the Maccabean brothers, his son John Hyrcanus (129–104 B.C.), and his grandson Alexander Jannaeus (104–76 B.C.). During this period there was an extension of Jewish rule over all the neighbouring countries and two of them, Edom and Galilee, were forcibly converted to Judaism. The area under Jewish control was now larger than in the time of Solomon.

But Jewish ideology does not easily conform to secular patterns, and the new powerful and prosperous state held within it the seeds of its own destruction. There was a hard core of Hebraism at the centre, and the old prophetic denunciations of the monarchy still rang in the ears of the people: 'Not by might, nor by power, but by my spirit, saith the Lord of Hosts.' When the Hasmoneans assumed the title of King as well as High Priest, and when later they began to behave in the manner of Hellenistic despots, they aroused opposition from the very section of the people which had helped them to power. These had originally called themselves Hassidim (the faithful or devoted) and they had refused to continue the struggle for political independence once religious freedom had been secured. Their more practical descendants, the Pharisaic party, aimed at both national and religious freedom, and for a time it seemed as though theocratic government, the consummation of their highest hopes, had actually been established.

Alexander Jannaeus, however, threw off all pretence of ruling according to prophetic standards and he deeply antagonized the Pharisees, the spiritual heirs of Hassidism, whose influence over the common people extended right up to the time of Jesus. The opposing party, called the Sadducees (from Zadok, the priest of Solomon), strongly supported the monarchy and the ecclesiastical tradition; much of the subsequent history of the Jewish state can be explained in terms of this ideological conflict.

When the Romans came on the scene (from 66 B.C.) the situation was so confused that they found no difficulty in applying their customary principle of 'divide and rule'. The divisions were already there, and some of the Pharisees actually pressed them to assume political control provided that the priesthood and the religious life of the people were left undisturbed. They acted at first with studied moderation, though Pompey is said to have offended the susceptibilities of the people by breaking into the Holy of Holies. The country was divided into four sections, Judaea, Galilee, Idumaea and Peraea, each with its own native ethnarch, a Roman nominee; Samaria and the coast-line were detached. The kingship was abolished but the ethnarch (or governor) of Judaea retained the high priesthood. This marks the end of Jewish independence, and henceforth, except for a short period (42 to 37 B.C.) when the Parthians from the east overran the country, the substance of power remained with Rome.

Soon the imperial rule became more hated than that of either Persian or Greek. This was partly due to the Roman habit of governing newly won countries by investing some local leader or chief with the full weight of their authority. The practice is familiar in modern times in the case of totalitarian states. In Judaea the ruling power seems to have been exceptionally favoured by fortune. Mention has been made of the conquest and forcible Judaizing of Idumaea, whose people (the Edomites, said to be descended from Esau, the brother of Jacob) were the inveterate foes of the Jewish people. Rarely in history has an act of intolerance had such a boomerang effect. Jannaeus had appointed a certain Antipater as governor of Idumaea; and it was through his successors, the second Antipater, his son, Herod the Great, and his grandson, Archelaus, that Rome exercised control, except for the brief Parthian interlude, until the sixth year of the Christian era. Whatever attempts these Idumaean princes made to exercise good government and win the favour of the people, they were regarded as the puppets of Rome and met with implacable hostility and resentment. This in its turn led to savage acts of retaliation, especially in the case of Herod, until finally, as a result of Jewish protests, Rome determined to make Judaea part of her own provincial system and appointed a series of procurators as governors. The fifth of these, selected by Sejanus (whose ruthless administration at Rome during Tiberius Caesar's retirement is so vividly described by Tacitus), was called Pontius Pilate.

This brings us to the contemporary scene in which Jesus lived. The Jewish people had already had a long history, consisting largely of a struggle for survival against overwhelming odds. They were now finally subjugated under the yoke of the most ruthless and efficient of all their foes. They still dreamt of becoming a free independent people with a ruler of their own stock who should exemplify in his government the principles laid down by their ancient teachers and sages. The origin and nature of that dream is the theme of the following chapter.

CHAPTER III

THE JEWS AS A RELIGIOUS PEOPLE

A N exceptional feature of Jewish history must already have
become clear: that one cannot study the social and political
development of this people without reference to their
religion. Much more than in the case of most nations the two
threads are inextricably interwoven.

All ancient peoples, it is true, attached importance to their
religion and believed that their fate was determined by the particular God or gods whom they worshipped. We even read of a
Moabite king who sacrificed his son and heir to Chemosh, the
tribal god, when he was defeated in battle (II Kings iii. 27). But
between them and the Hebrews there was a vital difference of
approach, a difference of kind rather than degree. This is best
illustrated by contrasting Hebraic with Greek ideas. In the
Homeric struggles the gods take sides and participate in the
fighting rather like aristocratic warlords; there is no suggestion of
a holy war or that 'rightness' belongs to a particular cause. Even
in historic times we do not feel that Hellas fought against Persia on
behalf of Zeus or Apollo – unless we take Apollo as the symbol of
the Greek way of life. The Greeks fought purely for political
autonomy against the encroaching waves of barbarism. The
Romans, too, were meticulous about omens, sacrifices and days of
public intercession. But their religion was an expression of national
discipline and their strength lay in the veneration they felt for the
majesty of Rome:

> . . . . whose course will on
> The way it takes, cracking ten thousand curbs
> Of more strong link asunder than can ever
> Appear in your impediment.

Such language could never have been used about the people of
Israel. The corresponding sentiment in their case would be:

28

Be still and know that I am God;
I will be exalted among the nations,
I will be exalted in the earth.
The Lord of Hosts is with us;
The God of Jacob is our refuge.

Nor do modern states exemplify this complete identification of
religion with national life. We pray for 'the peace of the realm' and
start our parliamentary sittings with intercession, but in general
we tend to think of the Church and religious practice as a 'special
department'. The Hebraic conception of life as sanctified action
does, indeed, occasionally possess us. But this spirit is only
spasmodic, and by a strange paradox it is the totalitarian countries
of today which offer the nearest modern parallel. For here, too, the
forms of political and social life are part of a total ideological
picture and the whole duty of the citizen is directed towards a
state ethical code.

This resemblance ceases, however, at the surface level, for the
Hebraic conception of life was dominated by the belief in one
all-powerful and transcendent God: a God who was indeed the
creator and sustainer of all mankind but with whom the Jews
thought of themselves as being in a special relationship. This was
the covenant relationship expressed in the familiar key-note that
rings right through the Old Testament: 'Ye shall be my people and
I will be your God.' But it was to be a relationship, not of privilege
but of service. By the whole character of their life as a community,
a life which knew no distinction between secular and religious,
they were to be God's witnesses to the rest of mankind.

It must not be thought that this pure monotheism, accepted as
a cardinal doctrine of faith by all Jews at the time of Jesus and even
many centuries before, was known to their earliest ancestors.
Indeed there is much in the early chapters of the Bible to suggest
that, like the peoples from whom eventually they came to stand out
as the worshippers of one God, the early Hebrews passed through
various stages of nature worship and polytheism. By the time of
the patriarchs they had reached the animist stage when trees,
streams, mountains, and so forth were regarded as the abode of
gods. Abraham, for instance, selected the turpentine tree at Mamre
for his altar. Jacob anointed a stone pillar at Bethel. The God whom
they came to regard as their own particular deity, and whose name,
Yahweh, is etymologically connected with the verb 'to be', may

well have been conceived as a god of thunder and storm, a *genius loci* who inhabited Mount Sinai.

Side by side with this nature worship there was a veneration for the family and the ancestral home. Like the Romans, the early Hebrews had their *penates*, 'household gods', which they transported as they moved from place to place. The *teraphim*, as they were called, were greatly prized. They play an important part in the stories of Rachel and Saul's daughter, Michal. Another feature of ancestor worship was the regard paid by ancient semitic families to the tombs of their dead. It is significant that the burial place of Moses was said to have been deliberately concealed lest it should become a centre of Hebrew worship.

The transition from this primitive form of religion to the later monotheistic Judaism came about gradually and through many successive stages. It was a long perilous voyage of adventure and discovery into the unknown world of the spirit. We are reminded of Virgil's *tantae molis erat Romanam condere gentem*. It was, indeed, a tremendous task to establish the supremacy of the Hebrew genius. The first stage was reached with the so-called Sinaitic revelation when Moses induced the people to make a covenant with Yahweh, and taught them that the essence of partnership was the recognition of mutual obligation. The life of a chosen people must be governed by principles acceptable to Yahweh and he, in his turn, would accord them his powerful protection. This way of life was embodied in a system of rules and regulations designed to achieve the total consecration of the community no less than of the individual. The earliest of such codes in Hebrew history, embodied in what are now universally known as the Ten Commandments or, in Hebrew, the Ten Words, and in the so-called Book of the Covenant (Exod. xx. 22–xxii), is traditionally associated with Moses and the Sinaitic revelation. Here we have the basis of the moral law and the belief in one God. The code was more humane, less draconian, than that of any other ancient people. Yet it is severe and, at times, even ruthless judged by modern standards.

For the bulk of the people were still primitive and unversed in the ways of civilization and, as Moses was well aware, the main deterrent against criminal behaviour was a superstitious fear of offending the supernatural power. Nor had they yet, except perhaps in the case of a few advanced thinkers, risen to the heights of a monotheistic conception. One of the earliest words used in Hebrew for God was a plural one, *Elohim*; and we read that as soon as Moses' back was turned at Sinai the people induced Aaron, his elder brother who acted as priest, to build them a golden calf before which they danced and shouted: 'These be thy gods, O Israel.'

During the period of the settlement in Canaan the temptation to abandon the worship of Yahweh in favour of his rivals in popular estimation, the Canaanite gods of fertility, was very strong indeed; for the Hebrews had still to learn that the God whom they associated with the storms and the solitary grandeur of Mount Sinai and with the period of their wanderings in the wilderness was in fact the Lord of the whole earth before whom the *Baalim*, as the Canaanite fertility gods were called, and their female counterpart (*Ashtoreth*) were less than 'the small dust of the balance'. Time and again we read of the Israelite kings who forsook the worship of the true God and followed after the Baalim, worshipping at their shrines or 'high places', the phallic pillars and the groves where their devotees carried out the various degraded rites of a heathen cult.

As their way of life became more settled, however, so did their worship of Yahweh begin to find expression in a more established form. Gradually there emerged a regular routine of sacrifice, divination and ritual meal. Certain days were set apart for family worship. The beginnings of the months and the seventh day of rest were consecrated. 'It is neither new moon nor sabbath', cries out the husband of the 'great woman' of Shunem in surprise when he sees her riding off to visit 'the man of God' (II Kings iv. 23). The establishment of the monarchy led to the building of what was first intended as a royal chapel but which quickly developed into the Temple, the central shrine which was the effective answer to the seductive temptations of the local high places. With the Temple there developed also the order of the priesthood. Independent guilds of a semi-religious character such as the 'Sons of the Prophets' appeared; one such guild, the Nazarites, devoted to ascetic forms of discipline, may be considered the prototype of the later Christian monastic system.

THE RISE OF THE PROPHETS

But the real opposition to the Baalim and the kings who so often supported their cult and 'did that which was evil in the sight of the

Lord' came, as we have already seen, from the Prophets. It was they who came increasingly to affirm that Yahweh was the one true God, not only of Israel but of all creation, and that what he required of man in addition to ceremonial worship and sacrifice was obedience to the moral law as expressed in human justice and social righteousness. The religious history of the period between the tenth and sixth centuries B.C. is the story of unceasing warfare between this pure conception of the deity and the superstitious and more degraded types of worship associated with idolatry and the Canaanite cults.

In that struggle each of the Biblical Prophets played his part, and through his native insight and vision added something fresh to that concept of God which was the unique contribution of his people's genius. Amos, who has been called the first social reformer, taught that God required of man a sense of social responsibility rather than correctness of ritual. His late contemporary Hosea emphasized the loving aspect of God and the redemptive influence of forgiving love. The 'holiness' of God, his demand of social righteousness from men in addition to ceremonial and sacrifice, is again the central doctrine of that statesman-poet, the first Isaiah. There followed the Josianic reformation which, as we have already seen, was an attempt to embody the teachings of the Prophets into a system of righteous living and humane government.

All subsequent 'prophecy' shows the influence of Deuteronomy and emphasizes or develops some aspect of Deuteronomic teaching. The appalling disaster of the Babylonian invasion in 586 B.C. and of the overthrow of Jerusalem set the seal to the warnings contained in this book that God would punish his people if they did not mend their ways. This is reflected especially in the message of the three great Prophets of the captivity period. Jeremiah and Ezekiel both emphasize aspects of the doctrine of personal responsibility. If God requires a righteous nation, this must start with the individual. Indeed Jeremiah, despairing of the seemingly vain hope of political righteousness at the national level, began to place an altogether new emphasis upon the centrality of personal religion. The former covenant between God and the people was to be superseded by a 'New Covenant' written not on 'tables of stone' but in the heart of the individual. The implications of this new doctrine were far-reaching indeed. For Jeremiah himself it involved the role not merely of prophet but of martyr. His insistence that his people should submit without resistance to the onslaught of the Babylonian invader was hardly likely to endear him to them or to command their acceptance. But it has made a profound impression upon the whole of the subsequent religious development of those peoples who have come under the influence of the Judeo-Christian tradition.

Less compelling, more practical and perhaps more superficial, was the teaching of Ezekiel. Already an exile himself he dreamed of 'the return' and of a theocracy in which the Temple was to be the centre of the restored nation and an elaborate priesthood were to act as mediators between God and his people. For the deity, so intimate in the mind of Jeremiah, was remote and majestic to this priest-prophet and could only be propitiated through self-abasement, or 'katharsis', expressed in terms of sacrifice and formal purification. Here we have the germ of what later became the established Jewish religion in its hierarchical aspect.

But the high-water-mark of Hebrew prophecy is reached in the later chapters of Isaiah, the unknown author of which is now generally referred to as 'Deutero-Isaiah'. Here the universalistic conception of God is expressed, not indeed for the first time but in the most unequivocal terms and in all the sonorous majesty of the Hebrew language: 'The Holy One of Israel is thy redeemer; the God of the whole earth shall he be called.' He is the creator of both darkness and light, evil as well as peace. All the events of history have been shaped by his hand; foreign nations and Israel alike are his special concern. Even in pre-captivity days, the first Isaiah could say, 'Blessed be Egypt my people, and Assyria the work of my hands'. But now an alien prince, Cyrus, is described as the Lord's 'anointed', as the messenger of God sent to carry out his will among the nations. He is to restore Israel to their native land where, as a newly constituted people, they are to play a special role in the divine economy.

Henceforth they will be a covenant-people, witnesses to the nations of God's creative power and of his concern for all created things. Thus their restoration is not to be for purely selfish ends. Moreover, for the first time in this remarkable story of religious development we find suffering beginning to be interpreted in terms of its vicarious effects, especially in the so-called 'Servant Songs' (Isaiah xlii. 1–4, xlix. 1–6, l. 4–9, lii. 13, liii. 12). Here the part of the elect people of God is seen as the often humiliating role of the scapegoat. They were to be despised and rejected by the nations, the chastisement of whose sins was to be upon them. But in the end their suffering would prove to be their glory and many transgressors would be turned to righteousness by it. The impact of this teaching upon the whole life and ministry of Jesus cannot be too strongly emphasized.

Subsequent prophecy, until we come to the ministry of Jesus himself, never quite rises to these heights. We have occasional echoes of the same passion for social righteousness and the same magnificent universalism, notably in Zechariah and Malachi, but gradually this particular literary form played itself out. Important religious developments did indeed take place among the Hebrews during the period between the Restoration and the birth of Jesus, but they are not so intimately associated (except in one case) with the character and vision of special personalities. They are therefore best treated by subject rather than chronology.

INSTITUTIONAL JUDAISM

The one exception was Ezra. The effect of his and Nehemiah's policy on the social history of the Jewish people has already been noted. But 'separatism' played a still more decisive part in their religious development. This can be best understood by a study of the account he gives of the first Passover celebration after the Return. The priests and Levites had purified themselves according to Levitical law and they had killed the Paschal lamb. Then comes the revealing phrase: 'And the children of Israel, which were come again out of the captivity, and all such as had separated themselves unto them from the filthiness of the heathen of the land, to seek the Lord, the God of Israel, did eat, and kept the feast of unleavened bread seven days with joy' (Ezra vi. 21–22).

Here we have a formulation of institutional Judaism. It was to be the religion of a 'peculiar' or separated people, a 'kingdom of priests and an holy nation'. It derived from God's revelation to 'his people' on Mount Sinai and the covenant by which they had bound themselves to act as his witnesses. It was a system of life and service combining the regulations of the priestly ceremonial law with the lofty ethical teachings of the Prophets.

The foundation of this system is best described by the Hebrew word Torah which, though narrowly interpreted as the 'Law', has in fact the much wider connotation of 'teaching' or 'instruction'. Throughout Jewish history it has been held traditionally to refer in particular to the so-called five books of Moses. Indeed in the canon of the Hebrew Bible as it eventually emerged these five books have always been known as the Torah. It was, in fact, from these books that Ezra read daily to the people, standing on a wooden pulpit, and thus inaugurated the service of the Synagogue. But the word in its more general, and at the same time more accurate, sense covered the oral or traditional Law as well as the written code. It stood for the whole corpus of precepts and interpretations handed down from father to son through centuries of Jewish scholarship.

Even in its narrower sense, however, the 'Law' bears traces of the work of many hands and of widely separated ages, and there is every justification for believing that some time after the Restoration the various fragments were woven together by priestly editors and presented as one continuous narrative. This in time came to be regarded in its entirety as the inspired word of God, and it was this that the later Jews 'grappled to their souls with hoops of steel'. It contained, so the Rabbis taught, no less than three hundred and sixty-five positive and two hundred and forty-eight negative precepts. Yet on these the devout among them based their every thought and their whole way of life; in defence of them they were prepared to die.

Such a compendium of ethics, ceremonial law and jurisprudence naturally required interpretation. There grew up a body of scholars, exegetes and jurists whose function it was to expound the Law to the ordinary people. Ezra himself was the first of these 'scribes', and he may therefore be regarded as the architect of the two main pillars on which subsequent Judaism rested, the Synagogue and the rabbinic school.

But there was another reason which accounts for the growth of these two institutions. From the time of the captivity the Jewish people were, as we have seen, widely scattered and this prevented them from taking part in the Temple worship. They could not, for instance, comply with the ordinance which bound them to appear before the Lord in Jerusalem three times a year at the harvest festivals of Passover, Pentecost and Tabernacles. The Temple, it is true, still remained the emotional centre of the Jewish people. The priests of Aaronic descent, together with their servants, the

Levites, still maintained the elaborate Temple ritual and the sacrificial system. Contributions of half a shekel each year were sent by loyal Jews living in the dispersion. But partly for geographical reasons, partly because the hierarchy became more and more involved in political controversy, the religious life of the bulk of the people was by the time of Jesus largely identified with the Synagogue and the Rabbis. In the previous centuries the Prophets had aroused the conscience of the whole people. Their successors were pious teachers who brought religion into the home.

It is not surprising, therefore, that there was a growth of individualism and that religious emphasis came to be placed on the leading of a pious life in conformity with the rules of Torah. At its best this meant 'prayer, fasting and almsgiving', at its worst a hollow compliance with customary ritual. Side by side with this were developments in theology. Some of these were characteristic of an individualistic age when large-scale national hopes have been abandoned and men are resigned to a life of subordination and suffering. Others were foreign importations from the lands contiguous to Palestine where so many Jewish families now lived as an integral part of the local population.

One side of this individualism showed itself in a growth of Jewish mythology, a form, according to modern psychologists, of intellectual escapism. Though not so rich as the Greeks in poetic imagery, both the Oriental nations, the Babylonian and the Persian, with whom the Jews had such close contact at this time, left their mark on Jewish views about the supernatural. Stories such as those of the Creation, the Fall of Man, and the Flood, though transformed into a monotheistic setting, owe their origin to Babylonian myth. This can be seen from a study of what remains of the seven clay tablets found in Asshurbanipal's library which contain the story of Marduk, the god of light, and his struggle with Tiamat, the dragon-goddess of chaos and darkness. Later Hebrew literature, moreover, shows a marked development of belief in angels and demons. Though some of these may be of native origin, the Genesis Midrash (see p. 48) and the Jerusalem Talmud both state that 'the names of the angels were brought by the Jews from Babylonia'. Judaism always remained uncompromisingly monotheistic, but the Hebrew literature of the last pre-Christian centuries shows the influence of Babylonian dualism and the elaborate demonology of the Zoroastrian system which was the basis of Persian belief. The conceptions of Satan as 'the tempter' or 'the adversary' in Job, Zechariah and the Book of Enoch, and of Asmodaeus, the evil spirit, in Tobit both illustrate this tendency. Further examples are the 'good' angels such as Gabriel, the 'messenger', and Raphael, who is described in the Book of Tobit as 'one of the seven holy angels which present the prayers of the saints and go in before the glory of the Holy One'.

For in an age of suffering when men felt the remoteness of God they sought to comfort themselves by the creation of intermediaries. There must be some method of human approach to the awful and majestic Being whose thoughts and ways were so different from the thoughts and ways of man. Hence arose a conception which had a profound effect on Jewish, and still more on Christian, religious thinking. We have seen how Greek influence permeated Judaea in the later Biblical age, especially after Alexander's conquest, and how it had left its mark on what is called the Wisdom literature of the Bible (Proverbs, Job, Ecclesiastes) and the Apocryphal writings of Ben-Sira and the Wisdom of Solomon. The use of the term 'wisdom' in this connection derives from the tendency of these authors to personify *chokmah* (the Hebrew word for wisdom). Ben-Sira, for example, identified it with the Law and regarded it as the instrument with which God created the world. This idea is carried still further by the author of the Wisdom of Solomon (first century B.C.) who links the Hebrew conception of wisdom with Plato's Logos, the divine reason or 'word of God'. 'Thine almighty word [Logos]', he writes, 'leaped down from heaven out of thy royal throne . . . and brought thine unfeigned commandment.' Here we get a conception of the 'intermediary' which found its fullest expression in the teachings of Philo, the Jewish philosopher of Alexandria at the time of Jesus, and in the prologue to the Fourth Gospel.

Individualism is always the enemy of national exclusiveness. There were two other expressions of religious feeling which were in part reactions from the particularist policy of Ezra and 'the men of the Great Synagogue', as his successors were called. One was a new and splendid universalism. It is found in such books as Ruth, a pastoral idyll, in which David, the ideal Jewish king, is shown as the descendant of Ruth the Moabitess, and Jonah where, to the discomfiture of a Jewish prophet, God shows compassion to Nineveh, the inveterate foe of Israel. Some of the lyrical poetry of the period (e.g. Ps. cxlv), including one beautiful romance, the Song of Songs, strikes the same universal note. Indeed, spiritual romance becomes a common feature of later Hebrew, and especially of what might be called the Daniel literature, written during the Maccabean period to give new hope to the people who suffered from the Seleucid persecution.

The second is the development of the literary form known as Apocalypse. This Greek word means an uncovering (i.e. of the future or latter end). Much earlier in history there had emerged the conception of the Day of the Lord, a day when mankind would receive final judgment and downtrodden Israel would rise to its rightful position as the people of God. The Prophets, notably Amos, had administered a stern rebuke to this easy optimism and had described the Day of the Lord as one of terror and darkness. Now through the influence of Zoroastrianism with its conception of four world periods of three thousand years each, much more elaborate pictures were drawn of future cosmic processes. It was not that the Jewish writers were less concerned with the fate of their people as that they gradually realized that their glorious destiny would never come about in the ordinary course of history. It would require the direct intervention of God himself. Hence the descriptions in the Apocalyptic passages (e.g. Isaiah xxiv, Daniel vii, Book of Enoch, etc.) are of supernatural and transcendent phenomena. Some of them are confidently eschatological and assert that the date of the end of days is fixed, and that it will not be long delayed.

Another Jewish religious concept whose influence on Jesus and his contemporaries can hardly be exaggerated was the belief in the coming of a Messiah. The Hebrew root from which this word is derived means 'to anoint'. Its later and religious connotation came from the practice of anointing with oil anyone (e.g. a king or priest) who was to be sanctified or specially marked out for the service of God. Even a heathen prince, Cyrus, as we have seen, is called 'my Messiah' by a Hebrew prophet of the captivity, for his task was to deliver God's people out of the hand of their oppressors. Gradually, however, the term came to be associated with the idea of a prince of Davidic descent who should establish Israel at the head of the nations and inaugurate an epoch when 'the mountain of the Lord's house shall be established at the top of the mountains and all nations shall flow unto it'. This conception coupled the spiritual supremacy of the Jewish people with an age of peace and prosperity for all men.

While it would appear that the figure visualized in the Messianic passages of the prophets is that of a human ruler, there emerged during the Hasmonean period another quite different figure of Apocalyptic literature, the 'Son of Man'. There is some doubt about the meaning of the title. In Ezekiel it is used simply to signify 'a frail child of man', or Adam; in the later Apocalyptic books (e.g. Daniel and Enoch) the Son of Man is a supernatural figure who appears in the clouds and receives dominion over all people in perpetuity. We may say that the Messiah came to be thought of as the ruler of the new kingdom in so far as it was to be brought about in history, while the Son of Man would be enthroned by the direct intervention of God. The latter conception was therefore more free from any particularist aspirations on the part of the Jewish people. It is most completely expressed in a book of the first century B.C., 'The Testaments of the Twelve Patriarchs'.

> Then shall the Lord raise up a new priest
> and to him all the words of the Lord shall be revealed;
> ... And his star shall arise in Heaven as of a king
> Lighting up the light of knowledge as the sun the day ...
> And there shall none succeed him for all generations for ever,
> And in his priesthood the gentiles shall be multiplied in knowledge
>   upon the earth,
> And enlightened through the grace of the Lord.
>
> Testament of Levi, xviii. 2–9.

One final problem exercised the minds of Jewish thinkers and poets in the period before the birth of Jesus, the problem of survival after death. Until this period there is little articulate in Hebrew writing on the subject, though it is clear from several passages that there was from very early times a generally held belief that some sort of shadowy life continued beyond the grave. This took place in a vast pit or underworld called Sheol, which both prophet and psalmist treat as a place of gloom, remote from the presence of God. We can infer also from the denunciations of the prophets that the practice of necromancy was common, and one Old Testament story describes the raising of Samuel's departed spirit from the dead by means of witchcraft. Recent archaeological work in Palestine, disclosing various utensils for food in the tombs, confirms the view that the Jews, like other ancient peoples, regarded some kind of personal survival as certain.

But the failure of earthly hopes and the conception of a final day of judgment brought this problem acutely before the minds of the later religious thinkers. Gradually the idea of personal resurrection took shape. At first it is closely related to the principle of retribution. At the Day of Judgment all the righteous will be raised from Sheol where the wicked are to remain for ever. Later we read in Enoch and the Psalms of Solomon that both good and bad will take part in a general resurrection. But nowhere until the first century of the Christian era is any clear distinction made between soul and body. By that time the influence of Platonic conceptions about man's imperishable soul and the Greek and Oriental mystery religions began to affect Jewish thought, and flowered especially in the syncretic genius of Philo. Thus arose the doctrine of the soul's immortality after the body had returned to dust. But before the age of Jesus the typically Hebraic emphasis on personality dominated all ideas of life after death among the Jews, just as it had permanently shaped their conception of the divine.

CHAPTER IV

RELIGIOUS LIFE AT THE TIME OF JESUS

IT must not be inferred from this cursory survey of the main trends of Jewish religious thought during the centuries before the birth of Jesus that all the beliefs described in the last chapter were held by the whole people at any one time. Totalitarian patterns of thought cannot exist among civilized nations unless they are subjected to extreme forms of indoctrination, and even then history shows that uniformity is as a rule short-lived. The Jews were by this time an exceptionally civilized people, and with characteristic independence of spirit they resisted all attempts at regimentation whether made by ruler or priest. This accounts for their somewhat turbulent history and for the wide variety of sects and parties into which they were divided during Jesus' lifetime.

Nevertheless there was a hard core of religious belief held by all Jews at this time, including Jesus himself. It rested on three cardinal doctrines whose origin was described in the last chapter. The first was the unity of God, who was revealed on Mount Sinai as creator and supreme ruler of the universe. The second was the selection of Israel as a covenant-people to proclaim his salvation to all the nations of the earth. The third was the truth of Torah, the inspired word of God which laid down the principles of all human morality as well as the special rules and laws by which Jewish life should be regulated.

But the Jews were essentially a practical people. No ancient code committed to writing at a definite period of history can meet the exigencies of all subsequent ages. This dilemma of divine perfection and practical necessity is one that faces all people who believe that God has revealed himself and declared his will in specific terms at a moment of time. The Jews met it in their own peculiar way. A tradition grew up among them that in the days of mourning for Moses 'three thousand rules were forgotten, whilst Joshua forgot another three hundred'. These rules were supplied by the Rabbis but, as was noted in the last chapter, even before their time there was developed what was known as the unwritten law, or oral tradition.

It was this conception of Torah which enabled the Rabbis to adapt or to expand an enactment of the original code to suit contemporary needs without invalidating its authority. A good example of their method in the time of Jesus is to be found with reference to the Law of Release (Deut. xv. 1–18). By the terms of this law all debts were remitted every seventh year – a well-intentioned but quite impracticable piece of legislation. Hillel, Jesus' great contemporary, invented a legal fiction called *prosbul*, by means of which a debt might be reclaimed at any time except during the year of Release; this prevented a debtor from making use of the law in order to keep his loan in perpetuity. Through devices of this kind many obsolete laws were silently abolished (e.g. *lex talionis*) without their being deleted from the statute book. Indeed, the Jews could not have survived in any other way; for their laws forbade them to fight on the Sabbath and it was only after a series of defeats that the Maccabees, on the principle that 'the Sabbath was made for man, not man for the Sabbath', found a way of circumventing the law and so enabled their armies to secure victory. They argued that Torah, which included Sabbath observance, was given to Israel for life, not for death. Yet these were the exceptions, and in the main the Jews of Jesus' time clung to the actual enactments of their code with a tenacity which could only spring from deep reverence and love.

There can be no doubt that adherence to Torah produced among the Jews a high standard of ethical conduct. The moral law was always held by Jewish teachers to be more important than the ceremonial: 'To obey is better than sacrifice.' Indeed, there were certain moral laws which were regarded as binding on all mankind, and in course of time the Rabbis came to formulate a code known as the Noachic laws. These were so called because all men were regarded as descendants of the three sons of Noah to whom the laws were given before the revelation to Israel on Mount Sinai. They related to (*a*) cruelty to animals, (*b*) blasphemy, (*c*) robbery, (*d*) murder, (*e*) idolatry, (*f*) immorality, and (*g*) the promotion of justice. But a specially high standard of morality devolved upon the Jewish people in view of their divine election. 'Ye shall be holy, for I the Lord your God am holy.' Justice, charity, love of one's neighbour, sexual purity – all this and much more was demanded of the Jew by his moral code, and if he often fell below these standards there is every reason to think that there was a higher and more humane level of conduct among this people than anywhere else in the ancient world.

This was at least partly due to the immense importance attached by the Hebraic mind to that other half of their code, the ceremonial law. To an intensely practical people like the Jews moral conduct did not seem possible without the observance of a strict form of ritual. Thus every part of a man's life was consecrated in conformity with the prescribed rules and regulations of religious ceremonial. At birth a Jewish boy was initiated into the covenant by circumcision, at thirteen he became *Bar Mitzvah* – that is, an adult member of the community or *Kelal Yisroel* who bound himself to undertake all the duties and obligations of Jewish Law. Marriage and death had their prescribed ceremonial, as well as the washing of the hands before meals and the breaking of bread. The essence of the whole was symbolized by the *mezuzah*, or container, by means of which a small piece of parchment inscribed with the verses from Deuteronomy vi. 4–9 was fixed on the right doorpost. These verses contain not only the basic theological affirmation concerning the nature of God – 'Hear, O Israel, the Lord our God is one Lord' – but also its immediate and far-reaching implication: 'And thou shalt love the Lord thy God with all thine heart, and with all thy soul, and with all thy might.' The applicability of both to every aspect of life is emphasized by what follows:

> And these words, which I command thee this day, shall be upon thine heart: and thou shalt teach them diligently unto thy children, and shalt talk of them when thou sittest in thine house, and when thou walkest by the way, and when thou liest down, and when thou risest up. And thou shalt bind them for a sign upon thine hand, and they shall be for frontlets between thine eyes. And thou shalt write them upon the door posts of thy house, and upon thy gates.

Every male wore a fringe (*tsitsith*) of blue and white on his outer garments and put on phylacteries, called in Hebrew *tephillin* (prayers), consisting of small leather cases containing the same words which could be bound with straps round his forehead and left arm as a daily reminder that these words should be on his mind and in his heart.

There was an elaborate sacrificial system centred on the Temple to which all males travelled for the three great festivals – Passover, Pentecost and Tabernacles. The beginning of the religious year (in Tishri, the seventh month) was marked by the blowing of the Ram's Horn on Rosh Hashanah (New Year) which summoned the people to a ten days' 'penitential season', culminating in the great fast called Yom Kippur, the Day of Atonement. On this one day in the year the High Priest entered the Holy of Holies in the Temple and, calling on God by name, made confession for the sins of the people.

But the most typical of all the Jewish institutions was that of the Sabbath. Other peoples could not understand this passion for compulsory rest and ascribed it, as Juvenal did in his sixth satire, to a love of idleness. But to the Jew the day epitomized all his feeling of love for God, who had rested on the seventh day after the creation and commanded him to 'call the Sabbath a delight', to put aside all worldly thoughts and occupations and devote himself to prayer and rejoicing of the heart.

The regulations regarding the Sabbath rest were indeed so rigorous as to be almost impossible of fulfilment by a civilized society. They were based on the Fourth Commandment which contained the injunction: 'Thou shalt not do any work thereon.' So categorical was the original interpretation of this verse that physical exertion and secular occupation of any kind were forbidden. The art of healing, for instance, could not be practised unless life was in danger. No fires might be lighted and no food cooked. In practice, however, a liberal interpretation was often placed on these regulations, which naturally lent themselves to casuistry and equivocation. To give an instance, if a man wished to visit a friend on the Sabbath who lived more than a Sabbath day's journey away (about three-quarters of a mile) he used to go to a spot within the required distance early on Friday before the commencement of the Sabbath and deposit there some bits of food representing two meals. He could then be regarded as living there on the principle that 'where a man's food is, there is his home'. In general, however, the Sabbath, in spite of its rigour, remained the greatest treasure in all the rich storehouse of Jewish religious observance; and even the Rabbis when prescribing its regulations were mindful of their own dictum: 'The Sabbath is given to you, not you to the Sabbath.'

Two other institutions on which the main structure of Judaism in Jesus' time rested were the Temple and the Synagogue. The former and more ancient of these was the centre of the state religion, or of what today we should call the Established Church. It was also the focus of national sentiment for a people who by this time were scattered all over the civilized world. The Synagogue was the home of a more personal, less spectacular, religion where the heart and mind of the individual worshipper found a fuller expression. The two were not antagonistic but complementary to each other.

The Temple as Jesus knew it had been rebuilt by Herod the Great in 20–19 B.C. after suffering serious damage from foreign invasion. The sanctuary itself, a building of about five hundred by one hundred and fifty feet was completed in eighteen months, but the outer courts were still being rebuilt in Jesus' lifetime (Mark xiii. 1, John ii. 20). Here an elaborate ritual of sacrifice was regularly maintained. There were processions accompanied by music, the singing of psalms, sometimes dancing. On Sabbath and festivals additional sacrifices were offered and special songs (such as the Deuteronomic Song of Moses) were sung. On Tabernacles, the most joyous of all the Jewish holy days, the celebration, consisting of music, procession and torch-dance, lasted all night. An early Rabbi said that he who had not taken part in the Tabernacles observance in Jerusalem had not lived.

This ritual and the general work of maintenance were in the hands of the priests, who claimed to be descendants of Aaron, with the High Priest in supreme control. They were divided into twenty-four panels or 'courses' who functioned in turn for a week at a time. Below them were the lower grades of the hierarchy, the Levites, the Asaphites (choristers) and Kohathites (porters or door-keepers). But in spite of this elaborate officialdom, the Temple worship was regarded in a special sense as a combined act of the whole people. It was the medium through which the whole house of Israel honoured their divine ruler. They could not for geographical reasons assemble as one man, and therefore sent representatives, known as 'standing men', who in twenty-four panels (like the priests) resided at Jerusalem for a week at a time and attended the Temple services. In this way the sanctuary retained its hold on the vast mass of the people who felt that they themselves directly participated in its ritual and were thus personally linked with the Shechinah, or divine presence (see p. 143).

That Judaism survived the final destruction of this elaborate system of Temple worship and the overthrow of the priesthood is one of the outstanding wonders of history. Nor is the reason far to seek. We have already seen how six centuries earlier, under the influence of Jeremiah and Ezekiel, the exiles in Babylon developed a ritual of prayer and praise which took the place of the Temple sacrifice. By the time of Jesus the people had become much more widely dispersed throughout the Roman Empire, with the result that the Synagogue rather than the Temple became for most Jews the natural centre of public worship. Synagogue is a Greek term meaning 'a gathering together'. In Hellenistic times it came to be used by the Jews as the equivalent of such earlier Hebrew expressions as *Beth Ha-Kenesseth* (House of Assembly) or *Beth Tephillah* (House of Prayer). The Synagogue was also regarded from early times as a house of study (*Beth Hamidrash*). Here, in every town and village of Palestine – there were, according to a tradition, over three hundred synagogues in Jerusalem alone – and throughout the Diaspora, the Jews gathered week by week on the Sabbath, and later day by day, to hear their beloved Torah read and expounded and to offer prayers to their Father in heaven, the giver of the Law. This was the institution that preserved the soul of Judaism and proved to be a bulwark alike against the foreign persecutor and the corrosions of time.

Gradually it evolved, as in the case of the Temple, an elaborate but much more homely ritual. In the time of Ezra the 'services' seem to have been confined to readings from the Law, which was in Hebrew, followed by an explanation or paraphrase in Aramaic, the language spoken by the ordinary people. This later developed into a discourse delivered by a man of piety and learning, the origin of our modern sermon. There was added a second scriptural passage, the Haphtorah ('conclusion') or reading from the Prophets, as well as the recital of certain prayers. The nearest approach to a credal affirmation was the recitation of the Shema, the famous passage from the sixth chapter of Deuteronomy with which were associated two cognate passages from the eleventh chapter and from the fifteenth chapter of Numbers. The oldest and most important of the prayers which is still in daily use in synagogues throughout the world is the Shemoneh Esreh, or Eighteen Benedictions.

An important development took place at the famous Synagogue

of Alexandria. Here it was necessary for the scriptures to be read in Greek as the congregation did not understand Hebrew. At some period in the third century B.C. it is said that seventy (or seventy-two) scholars undertook the task of translating the Hebrew Bible into Greek. There is a legend that, though shut up in seventy different cells, they all produced an identical version. A modern historian has commented that no such unanimity would have appeared if they had been working together! Hence appeared the Septuagint, which became the Christian form of the Old Testament until Jerome's Latin translation, the Vulgate, was adopted early in the fourth century A.D. It has had an immense effect on Biblical scholarship as it has provided alternative readings for many doubtful passages in the Hebrew text. In this way it can be seen how, owing to its ubiquity and consequent flexibility, the Synagogue supplied those practical and pervasive elements which enabled Judaism to grow into something greater and more lasting than a national cult.

THE RABBINIC TRADITION

So far we have examined those features of Judaism which were a central or integral part of the common faith held by the vast majority of Jews at the time of Jesus. But outside these essential practices and beliefs there was room for wide divergence and even the clash of violent controversy. A number of independent groups had grown up during the period between the Restoration and the beginning of the Christian era – the scribes, or scholarly lawyers, later known as Rabbis (teachers), the Pharisees, the heirs of the Chassidim, who had been the backbone of the resistance movement against Antiochus, and the priestly or conservative party, called the Sadducees. An examination of these in a little more detail, as well as of a number of others, will help us better to estimate the extent of the influence they exerted over the minds of Jesus and his contemporaries.

Towards the end of the pre-Christian era the 'canon' of the Hebrew Bible was fixed. By this is meant that of all the many books that were current at the time a certain number were selected as having a special divine sanction and authority. Yet their bibliolatry, as it has been called, never led the Jews (if we exclude some important minorities) into the extremes of literalism or textual illiteracy. From the first a fine scholarly tradition was evolved, and though some of the scribes and 'writers', whose task it was to reproduce the books of the Law, were, like some modern printers, imperfect craftsmen, as a rule they brought a highly developed critical faculty as well as a devout sense of service and veneration to the performance of their task. It is largely to them that we owe the magnificent text of the Old Testament in current use among the three great monotheistic religions of today.

The Rabbis who succeeded them had the task of expounding the teachings of the Law and the Prophets and applying them to the practical needs of the people. It is important to remember that in the minds of the Jews there was no real distinction between what we should call the secular and the religious. The concept of the unity of all life followed naturally from the belief in the unity of God, and it was as natural for the Bible to deal with questions of social contract and legal administration as with the heights and depths of spiritual experience. The Rabbis therefore had to be civil lawyers as well as teachers of religion. They administered the local courts of law (the Beth Din or 'House of Judgment'; Greek, Sanhedrin) connected with the local synagogue as well as the supreme Sanhedrin at Jerusalem (see p. 62). The decisions of these courts and the records of the discussions upon which the decisions were based came gradually to be codified, and in the year A.D. 200 one of the greatest of all the Rabbis, Judah the Prince, published the Mishnah (or 'repetition') which was really the codification of the principal discussions and decisions which had been preserved to that time. This Mishnah became the subject of further study and discussion, and eventually in A.D. 500 in Babylon there was published a vast commentary (Gemarah) on the Mishnah which contained the wisdom, jurisprudence, folk-lore, homily and legend of the Jewish people for a considerable period of its post-Biblical history. This encyclopaedic compilation of the text of the Mishnah with the rabbinic commentary was known as the Talmud. It is to this literature as well as to the later commentaries on the Bible itself known as the Midrashim (enquiries) that we owe most of our knowledge of the religious and social life of the Jews at the time of Jesus.

So well did the Rabbis do their work that they earned not only the respect but also the affection of the bulk of the people. (Rabbi means 'my teacher' and the title preserves something of the original relationship.) They sprang from the people and were in no way,

like the Temple priests, a privileged caste. Yet they were treated
with great courtesy and became a kind of intellectual aristocracy.
They sat in the chief seats in the Synagogue; no family function was
complete unless graced by the presence of one of them; to marry a
Rabbi's daughter, even to perform some menial function for him,
was regarded as a cherished privilege. Something of the veneration felt for Jesus by his contemporaries was due to the rabbinic
quality in him and because he taught 'as one having authority'.

Nevertheless this veneration had its dangerous side and the
Rabbis were sometimes prone to a certain intellectual arrogance
and even spiritual pride. Neglect of study of the Law always earned
their special condemnation and, as we shall see later, their attitude
towards the simpler farming folk (Am-ha-aretz – people of the
land, peasants, as we should say) was one of extreme contempt. But
there were many types of Rabbi at the time of Jesus and it is
unsafe to generalize. At their best they were like Hillel, a man of
sincerity, gentleness and courtesy. But there was also to be found
in their ranks the religious pedant who stuck to the letter of the
law, as well as the quibbler who strained the meaning of language
to suit his purpose. The well-known story of Hillel and Shammai
illustrates these divergencies. A Gentile once approached the
severe Shammai, saying that he would become a proselyte if the
Rabbi would teach him the whole Law while he stood on one foot.
Shammai flew into a rage and drove the man out with a measuring-
rod. He then went to the gentle Hillel who replied: 'What is
hateful to you do not to your fellow: that is the whole Law; all the
rest is commentary.' Such a reply, though it cannot be considered
as typical of the whole rabbinic outlook, springs from that lofty
conception of man's duty to God, and therefore to his fellow man,
which was the foundation of rabbinic teaching.

THE SECTS

Among the rank and file those most closely akin to the Rabbis
in spirit were the sect known as the Pharisees. The origin of the
name is obscure. Its most likely meaning is 'separatists' and it was
probably a term of abuse used by their opponents, the Sadducees,
about those who maintained that the oral law had an equal
validity with the written one. It is unfortunate for their reputation
in history that the best known passages about them in contemporary literature were written by those who had reason to dislike

them. A similar fate has befallen the Jesuits and, as usual in such cases, early emotional prejudice has left its mark on our vocabulary. It is now generally conceded that the words Pharisaic and Jesuitical do less than justice to the two orders which they affect to describe.

The Pharisees were indeed the sincerest elements of the population. They formed themselves into fraternities who attempted to put rabbinic doctrine into practice and to lead lives which combined meticulous observance of the forms of religion with extreme inner piety. They made no claim to privilege but imposed on themselves the severest obligations. The historian Josephus (who was of a noble priestly family and had no particular reason to love them) says that they were much more popular than the Sadducees. Indeed, they were of the people and the beliefs they held were those which had a popular appeal and offered comfort and consolation to a suffering age. They laid great emphasis on repentance and the everlasting mercy of God, who was ever ready to receive the sinner. For man according to rabbinic teaching was a free creature, but he was constantly being pulled in opposite directions by the *Yetser ha-Tob* (good inclination) and the *Yetser ha-Ra* (evil inclination). They looked forward eagerly to the coming of a Messiah. They accepted the traditional demonology (see p. 36) and believed in the resurrection of the dead and divine judgment after death. In spite of their puritanical strictness about observance of the Law they were eager to make proselytes among the Gentiles. Their best teachings are summed up in a book called 'The Testament of the Twelve Patriarchs', probably written by a Pharisee of liberal views about 105 B.C. He taught that the Law was given to lighten man's burden, that the Gentiles would be saved, and that man's duty consisted in love of God and one's neighbour.

Thus the Pharisees expressed what was best and most enduring in Judaism and it was, as we shall see, with these men that Jesus had the closest affinity. One section of them, indeed, probably supplied his first followers and became the nucleus of the early Christian Church. These we may call the Apocalyptic Pharisees, for they emphasized the supernatural element in the Messianic belief and looked for an immediate sign of deliverance from heaven. Josephus tells us that they were always urging the people to follow them into the desert and mentioned two 'false prophets', Theudas and a certain Egyptian, who were put to death by the

Roman Governor after their promises to perform certain miracles
had proved a delusion.

But the main Pharisaic emphasis was on conduct and it was
their scrupulous adherence to rule and rite that laid them open to
the charge that they made a parade of religion. There is always a
tendency among ordinary people to judge those who aspire to
virtue on a highly exacting basis, whereas self-confessed sinners
and the 'weaker brethren' are let off on comparatively easy terms.
In the case of some Pharisees the principle *corruptio optimi
pessima* did certainly apply. Formalism may easily lead to ostentation and spiritual pride. Strict observance of dietary and other
rules often involves segregation, from which may arise contempt
for the more lax, the 'lesser breeds without the law'. 'I am not of
your element' says the puritan Malvolio to the lighter members of
Olivia's household, and those Pharisees who 'made broad their
phylacteries' may have thought in those terms of the less devout,
and particularly of the Am-ha-aretz. There is even a passage in
the Talmud which speaks of the plague of Pharisaism and con-
temptuously divides them into seven categories or grades of which
only one was 'Pharisees from love'. Yet all this must not blind us
to the fact that from their ranks came the exponents of the loftiest
form of Judaism, and that if some of them displayed the uglier
features of a formal religion it was because their aim was one which
man has always found it most difficult to achieve – the possession
of a humble and contrite heart.

Their opponents, the Sadducees, made no such lofty pretensions, and in consequence posterity has been much fairer to them.
They were the wealthier and more privileged class who supported
the priesthood and resided chiefly at Jerusalem. They were on
friendly terms with Herod and the Roman administration and
opposed any popular attempts to overthrow them and establish an
independent state. Religiously they may be called reactionaries or
purists who stuck to the literal text of scripture and rejected all
the additions and valuable modifications which had emanated from
the rabbinic schools. They had no belief in the immortality of the
soul or the existence of angels, nor much faith in the coming of the
kingdom of God. In a sense they were the first existentialists, for
they concentrated on the life of this world and advised man to
eschew long hopes and regulate his life according to prescribed
rules. They were satisfied with the existing state of things and

their worldly teaching had little influence on a Messianic-minded people whose whole vision was coloured by 'immortal longings'.

At the opposite end of the scale was a small semi-monastic group called the Essenes. They are not mentioned in the New Testament or the Talmud and we do not know the Hebrew word for them. Our information comes chiefly from Josephus who for a time had lived amongst them. They numbered, he tells us, about four thousand. Their aim was to live a life free from worldly contamination and corruption, and in order to achieve this they practised extreme forms of asceticism. They lived in scattered communities along the Jordan or in the hill country towards the Dead Sea. Ritual purity was symbolized by frequent bathing and it is generally held that John the Baptist was one of their sect. They took the command 'Thou shalt not kill' literally and lived on a strictly vegetarian diet. Some of them, like the Albigenses, of whom they frequently remind us, refused all sexual intercourse, though children might be adopted; those that married cohabited only for the purpose of having children. All property was held in common, the rich who joined their order giving their wealth into the common fund. They lived a life of hard work and service, cultivating the land of the settlement or practising the manual arts. Unlike the Pharisees they had little interest in the corporate life of Israel, but their outlook and practice seem to have had a marked effect on the earliest Christian communities.

This appears to be particularly true of a quasi-Essenic sect known as the Sons of Zadok (or New Covenanters) of whom more and more is becoming known since the discovery of the 'Zadokite Document' in 1896 and the Dead Sea Scrolls in 1947. They may have sprung originally from the same source as the Sadducees (hence the term Zadokite), but by the time of Jesus the two groups were totally dissimilar both in outlook and practice. The evidence shows that they were a group of saintly ascetics whose whole life was based on the strictest rules of conduct collected in a 'Manual of Discipline'. Membership could only be obtained through the most elaborate initiation ceremonies. They accepted the ordinary beliefs of Judaism, with an emphasis on its mystical (or cabbalistic) elements, and in particular looked forward to the return to earth of their founder, a Teacher of Righteousness who had been put to death by a 'wicked priest'. Some of them seem to have fled to Damascus, possibly as a result of Roman persecution, and there to have awaited this event as a prelude to the coming of the Messiah.

The exact relationship between this sect and the early Christian Church is difficult to determine. For one thing, not all the Scrolls have yet been deciphered or translated. And for another, scholars are still far from agreeing as to the date of their composition. The most probable view is that they belong to the first century B.C. and that the teaching and practice of the sect they describe foreshadowed to some extent the advent of Christianity. One scholar goes so far as to identify the Teacher of Righteousness with Jesus himself, but there is no evidence to show that Jesus had any contact with the Essenic groups. There is little doubt, however, that the early Christian Church drew some of its support from their ranks.

Far more politically-minded, far less concerned with the things of the spirit, was the fourth and last group of those into which the Jewish people of Jesus' time were divided. These were the Zealots (Kannaim) or adherents of the Fourth Philosophy, as Josephus calls them. With the Jews, religion was rarely divorced from political implications, and the Zealots believed that it was impossible to be a true worshipper of God and at the same time submit to Roman domination. Their movement took shape when a Galilean named Judas urged his countrymen not to pay taxes which the Roman ethnarch Quirinus had imposed as the result of a census taken in the year A.D. 6. Galilee had long been the scene of disorder and rebellion and the father of Judas, a certain Hezekiah, was earlier put to death by Herod the Great for organizing plunder and rapine on a large scale throughout that province. Judas's first rebellion, which took place at Herod's death, was quickly suppressed, but by means of a kind of underground movement he was able to terrorize not only the Roman officials but many of those Jews who acquiesced in Roman dictation. At one time they seem to have secured the support of that section of the Pharisees who followed Shammai. Later they earned for themselves the title of *sicarii* (dagger-men) or *lestai* (robbers), but we must remember that Josephus, our chief authority, was a 'fellow-traveller' where Rome was concerned and his judgment may be warped with prejudice. They were in all probability misguided religious fanatics. The sentiment expressed by one of them does not seem to be lacking in sincerity: 'Moreover, I believe that it is

God who granted us this favour, that we have it in our power to die nobly and in freedom.'

Such was the complex religious scene in which Jesus spent his boyhood. Its most characteristic features were uncertainty, disunion, and a kind of restless expectancy. Of all the paradoxes of this paradoxical people none is stranger than this blend of implicit faith in divine providence and bitter dissension at the human level. As we shall see from the next chapter, the social and political conditions only aggravated the general feeling of restlessness which prevailed among all but a very small section of the population.

CHAPTER V

SOCIAL AND POLITICAL LIFE AT
THE TIME OF JESUS

IF restlessness was a dominant characteristic of the Jewish
people in the age of Jesus it cannot be accounted for in religious terms alone. Men's beliefs about God and ultimate truth
are always shaped to some extent by the political, economic and
social forces which control their everyday lives. We cannot begin
to get a clear picture of the thoughts and motives which were
working in the minds of Jesus and his contemporaries unless we
realize that Palestine was what might be called an occupied
country. Not only were the people without political power, but
for centuries they had grown accustomed to the sight of foreigners
– Greek mercenaries, Parthian horsemen, Roman officials and
legionaries – living in the outskirts of their villages and liable to
make a sudden entry into their houses. It is true that the powerful
Hasmonean dynasty had given them a short period of political
independence. But this had only whetted their appetites for more;
right through the hated reign of Herod and the subsequent rule of
the Roman procurators the religious expectancy, noted in the last
chapter, constantly took political shape. People looked for a
national saviour who, as a preliminary to establishing the Kingdom
of Heaven, would throw off the hated Roman yoke.

Nevertheless it was not the Roman custom to interfere with the
patterns of social life which they found among the peoples whom
they conquered and, though they could not be expected to understand the strange Jewish obsessions about the divine, they left
their highly civilized ways and practices largely undisturbed. These
centred on the family for, at least from Prophetic times, the Jews
had been monogamistic and the position of women among them
was considerably higher than was usual in the ancient world. We
can tell this from innumerable Biblical stories, ranging from those
about Deborah and Esther down to the contemporary pictures of
women such as Martha and Priscilla. There was deep affection for
children and the home, and the whole picture of the family life

given in the Book of Tobit is one of warmth and intimacy. When Jesus asked his followers to leave their homes he was making great demands on them, and adopting a tradition which belonged only to the small Essene sect and was off the beaten track of Jewish life.

There was a wide variety of trades and occupations. Since their original settlement in the fertile crescent the Jews had been an agricultural people, and ever since the disappearance of the northern kingdom (722 B.C.) Judea had consisted of a single important town, Jerusalem, surrounded by a network of villages. But from the time of the Ptolemies great encouragement was given to industry and commerce; towns began to grow up all over Palestine and particularly along the coast. Mines were opened for iron and copper, the art of building was learned from the Phoenicians, there were carpenters, masons, smiths, even manufacturers of rich jewels and musical instruments. Different parts of the country specialized in different industries; Galilee, for instance, was famous for its corn and the town of Taricheae became the centre of the lake fisheries. The different trades often formed themselves into guilds, the members of which were pledged to mutual support. The whole country therefore throbbed with a busy life and there was a great feeling for the dignity of manual labour. 'There is no trade', said the Rabbis, themselves craftsmen, 'which the world can spare.' And again: 'Where a man teaches his son no trade, it is as if he taught him highway robbery.'

But, as always happens when there is a rapid growth of urban population, deep cleavages in society began to appear. The townspeople, though not rich by modern standards, became wealthier than the country folk. And what was of more consequence in a Jewish cultural setting, they had greater opportunities of study and religious observance and came to despise their agricultural neighbours, the Am-ha-aretz (people of the land), as country boors. (The word 'pagan', derived from the Latin *paganus*, 'countryman', offers a good parallel.) Tensions between these two classes arose partly, too, from economic causes. According to Biblical law the priests and Levites were supported by the tithes paid by the farmers on their produce. The town-dwellers, or Haberim as they were called, were exempt from such taxation and this increased the farmers' resentment. They sometimes went so far as to refuse to pay the tithe, and we read of cases where the priests sent their slaves to exact it by force; normally, however, they met the difficulty by increasing the price of grain sold to the consumer, and in later times the purchaser himself had to pay the tithe as the farmer's word could not be trusted. All this produced great bitterness which, especially in Galilee where the bulk of the people were Am-ha-aretz, often expressed itself in revolutionary demands for social equality.

'The poor shall never cease out of the land', wrote the Deuteronomist, and his words were more than justified by the extreme poverty which was the common lot at the time of Jesus. Years of wars and devastation had left their mark; except for a few very rich, most of whom were foreigners or Jews working for the administration, the people lived in the simplest possible way and it was a struggle to provide the barest subsistence. The average wage of a labourer might be, as in one of the stories of Jesus, a denarius (about ninepence) a day, and the rent of a small village house varied from about seven to twenty-eight shillings a year. Luxury was unknown except in the houses of a few rich people and the diet was largely vegetarian. When Hillel, the famous Rabbi, came to Jerusalem he worked for half a denarius a day. Out of this he had to support a family as well as bribe the steward of the rabbinic academy to allow him to attend the course of lectures.

Some of this poverty may have been alleviated by almsgiving. The Hebrew word for righteousness (*zedakah*) also meant charity, and the Rabbis taught that 'through alms a man partaketh of eternal life'. Some Jews who wanted to acquire a reputation for piety made a public display of their charity. They are severely rebuked by Jesus (see Matt. vi), yet he does not hesitate on occasion to ask that those who wished to become his disciples should first sell their property and distribute the proceeds among the poor.

There was even a grade below that of intense poverty, namely slavery, but this was not as common among the Jews as among other peoples of the ancient world. It is improbable that the practice of selling debtors into bondage lasted till the time of Jesus (the parable in Matthew xviii may refer to Roman customs), but there is evidence that slaves, drawn largely from the descendants of the old Canaanites and other surrounding tribes, were employed in Jewish households. Nevertheless they met with none of the harsh treatment which was their normal lot in other countries. The Pharisees opposed the whole system of slavery, while the Essenes rejected it altogether. A saying in the Talmud shows that at least the Rabbis were aware of the inhumanity of the practice: 'Beware of eating fine bread thyself and giving thy servant black; or of sleeping thyself on cushions, whilst he lies on straw, especially when he is thy countryman and fellow-believer; for he who takes a Hebrew slave sets at the same time a master over himself.'

'THINE, O LORD, IS THE KINGDOM'

We have seen that Jewish parents took the greatest care of their children, who all received a form of education from their infancy. This, as we should expect, was religious in character, and its aim was to see that children were well grounded in the laws and traditions of their people. Lessons started in the home where the child learned to repeat short verses from the scriptures, beginning with the Shema, which is really the quintessence of Judaism. He would afterwards attend Synagogue and the Synagogue school, where he would hear readings from the Hebrew Scroll and perhaps receive special instructions from the local Hazzan whose function it was to read the services. In a backward country like Galilee the educational system would be far less developed than in Jerusalem, though we know that Jesus, who spoke the ordinary Aramaic language of the people, was able to stand up in the synagogue at Nazareth and read the difficult text of the sacred Scroll. The passion for learning which grew up in the Talmudical age is well illustrated by the story of how three Rabbis were sent to inspect the schools of Palestine. When they came to the first city they said to the leading citizens: 'Bring forth the guards of this city.' The citizens arranged for a parade of the local militia. 'These', replied the Rabbis, 'are not the defenders of your city, they are its destroyers. It is your teachers who are the true guards of your city.'

This respect for education had its roots in the period well before the birth of Jesus. 'Our chief care', writes Josephus, 'is to educate our children well.' And again: 'Our law commands us to bring our children up in learning and to exercise them in the laws, and to make them acquainted with the deeds of their forefathers that they may imitate them.' As always, the emphasis is on knowledge of the scriptures, Jewish ordinance and Jewish history. There is no interest in the wider disciplines that were engaging the mind of the contemporary Graeco-Roman world, science, philosophy, and the arts of poetry and rhetoric. But from his purer, if narrower stream of wisdom, the Jewish child could draw a deep understanding of God's ways and of how men should live a practical life in accordance with his will.

In the social and religious spheres, then, the Jews were able to preserve their accustomed forms and pursue their way more or less undisturbed. But contemporary records agree that the Roman administration brought with it one imposition which was apt to make the life of even the meanest cottager a misery. It was in the shape of a human pest known by the Latin word *publicani* – tax-gatherers. The general policy adopted by Rome for raising revenue from her provinces was to lease out the farming of taxes by contract to Roman officials. The companies engaged in this lucrative task had grown immensely rich and powerful and formed the backbone of what was known as the Equestrian order. But in Palestine the system seems to have been different. Here the taxes were paid direct to the government, the 'publicans' being local agents employed by the Roman officials. There were many types of payment which they were responsible for exacting, chief among which were the land tax and the capitation or poll tax. It was also their duty to assess all goods going in or out of a town and demand a quota for Roman use (see Matt. ix. 9). Their calling naturally provoked hostility which often turned to hatred. Some of them, no doubt, resorted to extortion and blackmail in order to wring an extra penny out of their unfortunate victims. Many were plainly dishonest and used their powers to enrich themselves. But in the eyes of the Jews they were something more hateful still; they were regarded as collaborators with Rome, disloyal to their nation and its religion. They were therefore branded as 'gentiles' and sinners and ostracized from Jewish society, and it required a good deal of courage to consort with them and treat them with any show of friendliness.

To understand the political administration of this 'occupied' country it is important to remember that after Pompey's conquest the country was split up into tetrarchies which retained a measure of independence. Some parts (e.g. Samaria) were entirely confiscated. Herod the Great was strong enough to unite the country for a time under his personal rule, but after his death in 4 B.C. it was again split up, this time into three parts under his three sons. Of these Antipas (the Herod of Luke) received Galilee and Peraea,

Philip the hill country in the north-east of Palestine, Archelaus, with the title of Ethnarch, Judaea, Samaria, and Idumaea. But such was the effrontery and oppressive conduct of Archelaus that Judaea and Samaria soon sent a joint embassy to Rome asking for his removal. The Emperor Augustus immediately decided to banish him and place his ethnarchy under Roman administration; so it came about that when Jesus was still a child, though his own native Galilee remained under the nominal rule of an Idumaean prince, Judaea, including Jerusalem, passed into the control of a Roman procurator.

It is interesting to see how even in the case of this turbulent people the Romans tried to carry out their habitual practice of 'imposing the custom of peace'. The procurators had their residence well away from Jerusalem at Caesarea, where they kept the bulk of their army. A small force (one cohort) was stationed at the capital, which these governors visited only at the time of the festivals. They did not interfere with the religious life of the people, and whenever the legionaries entered Jerusalem they scrupulously avoided carrying standards with the image of the Emperor on them, out of deference to Jewish susceptibilities. It was true that they appointed as High Priest a 'safe' man who could be relied upon to support them, and they maintained supervision over the sacred vestments, but in this they were only carrying on the practice of Herod the Great. In regard to the administration of justice a good deal of power remained, as we shall see, with the local tribunals, though the procurators assumed jurisdiction over political crimes. In a word, the Romans carried out a system of government that had proved highly effective elsewhere. Yet in Judaea, so far from producing a contented people and settled conditions, they aroused the bitterest resentment and hostility, which from time to time broke out into open insurrection.

The reason for this will be clear from much that has been said in the foregoing pages. In Jewish eyes administration and what we call politics were inextricably bound up with their religious faith. 'Thine, O Lord, is the kingdom and the power . . .' That is the recurrent theme which, with variations, runs right through Jewish history. But how could the average unimaginative Roman to whom religion was a state department, a matter of imperial loyalty, understand such an illogical, fanatical outlook? How could a Quirinus or any other Roman official realize that when he took a census of the people for purposes of taxation, his action would be interpreted as one which not only threatened fresh financial burdens but also repeated a crime for which centuries ago the people had been punished by plague (II Sam. xxiv)? No wonder that when they saw Rabbis and Pharisees actually preaching sedition and joining in acts of violence they mistook the Jewish religion for a degraded form of superstition which invoked some kind of magic against their authority and throve on political agitation. No wonder that they came to regard those who upheld it as the 'enemies of the human race'.

This attitude, no doubt, was responsible for the appointment in A.D. 26 of one of their most ruthless officials, Pontius Pilate, as procurator of Judaea. Of this man Philo, in his 'Embassy to Caius', says that he utterly lacked human compassion and would actually torture men to death without trial. Roman magistrates were never particularly squeamish in their methods of imposing discipline, but this man seems to have gone out of his way to offend Jewish susceptibilities. On one occasion he violated the Roman principle of non-interference in religious matters by moving his soldiers from Caesarea to Jerusalem and issuing orders that they should enter the sacred city carrying their standards stamped with the image of the Emperor. He was compelled to withdraw them through the stubborn and intrepid behaviour of the Jewish deputation which came to protest against this piece of wanton sacrilege. On another occasion he raided the Temple treasury in order to repair an aqueduct. When a crowd collected round his tribunal in angry resentment he sent his soldiers amongst them disguised as citizens and large numbers were wounded or trampled to death. It is not surprising that he was dismissed by the Roman government in A.D. 36.

But not all the Roman governors acted with such ruthlessness; generally speaking, unless they felt that their authority was being threatened they allowed the life of the people to pursue its normal course. This does not mean that they refrained from extortion or that they hesitated to enrich themselves at the common people's expense. Indeed the constant visits of the hated publican as well as the proximity of the soldiers was a continuous reminder of Roman domination. Nevertheless, in many important spheres of life (as we have seen in the case of religion and education) the people were more or less free to act as they liked. This is particularly true, except where political crimes were concerned, of the administration of justice.

THE SANHEDRINS

The main instrument of the judicial system in the time of Jesus was, as we have seen, the local tribunal or Beth Din (House of Judgment), better known by its Greek name, Sanhedrin. Its origin may be traced to the old council of elders instituted by Moses in the wilderness to share with him the burden of judicial responsibility (see Exod. xviii). The term Sanhedrin has been much misunderstood in subsequent ages, and even today it is often used as if it denoted a single court which met at Jerusalem. In fact there were Sanhedrins in all the towns and villages of Palestine, varying in composition from seven to twenty-three members. Three of the larger Sanhedrins met in Jerusalem.

These courts gave judgment in civil cases such as those arising out of contract, and criminal prosecutions, too, were brought before them, though the more serious cases were referred to the larger courts, some of which seem to have had power of capital punishment. Josephus tells us that when Herod was Governor of Galilee he was brought to trial before the Sanhedrin of twenty-three in Jerusalem, which dealt with cases of murder. He had ordered the execution of a robber chief, Hezekiah, father of Judas (see p. 53), whose family clamoured for revenge. The Jewish court, however, acquitted him. This may have been because according to Jewish law a man could not be convicted of murder unless he had done the killing with his own hand; but more probably the court were overawed by Herod, who carried with him letters from the Roman Governor of Galilee to King Hyrcanus II soliciting the royal protection. The right of this court, however, to inflict capital punishment is nowhere called in question.

Side by side with these local tribunals were the religious courts composed of the officers of the Synagogue. These met to consider breaches of the ceremonial law and gross violations of the recognized moral standard. They held powers of excommunication from the life of the Synagogue and in certain cases actual chastisement could be administered. The principles on which they judged were contained in what was called *Halachah* (oral law); this was fixed and interpreted by the most important of the religious courts, the Sanhedrin of seventy-one which sat in Jerusalem.

This Sanhedrin was a purely legislative body and, though in theory it held certain judicial rights (e.g. the trial of the High Priest, a false prophet, or a seceding tribe), these had fallen into abeyance and were never exercised after the first century B.C. The court had therefore no power to condemn to death. But it was the supreme religious authority not only over Judaea but over all the Jewish communities of the then known world; it decided on matters of Jewish law, regulated the calendar and ministered generally to the spiritual needs of the people. Like the Sanhedrin of twenty-three it was dominated by Pharisaic influence at the time of Jesus and among its presidents (*Nasi*) was the gentle Hillel.

It is often confused with a court of law which was summoned from time to time to try political offences. The evidence for the existence of this court, which we may call the *political* Sanhedrin, is scattered about the pages of Josephus. It was an *ad hoc* assembly appointed by the ruler of the state and composed of men who were likely to pronounce verdicts in accordance with his wishes. It was, as we should expect, Sadducean in character and, like the Star Chamber of English history, an instrument for carrying out the will of the executive power. It had no definite place of meeting and, unlike the religious Sanhedrin, could be summoned on any day of the week, Sabbaths and festivals included. When Judaea became a Roman province, we may be sure that the members of this court were chosen for their pro-Roman sympathies, men who could be relied upon to prosecute in all cases of supposed subversive activity. It was probably, as we shall see, this court which brought Jesus to trial, as well as his brother James and the first leaders of the Christian movement.

Such were the main features of social and political life in Palestine at the time of Jesus. It is a complex picture and shows the state of restlessness resulting from the 'clash of mighty opposites' within the narrow confines of a small country. In the power sense the conflict between Roman and Jew was an unequal one, but in the ideological sense the two combatants were more evenly matched. On the face of it, it might be thought that there was no incompatibility between them, that each had a contribution to make which was complementary to the other. After all the Romans had been successful elsewhere in bringing peace, security and a good administration to the turbulent and undisciplined peoples whom they conquered. They scrupulously refrained from interfering in the life and customs of these peoples and were the first great power in history to introduce the principle of tolerance into the art of government. Nowhere is this better illustrated than in their treatment of the Greeks. Here, too, they came across an ideology with which they were unfamiliar and which represented a challenge to their whole way of life. Yet they quickly recognized its worth and were able to make such mental adjustments as rendered it possible for Rome to act as the protector of Greek civilization. Why was this not possible in the case of the Jews?

The answer is that the incompatibilities were fundamental. The minimum demands made by Rome on her subjects were the acceptance of constituted authority and a respect for man-made law. These derived from an inherent sense of discipline which seemed to them a prerequisite for any ordered form of life. To the Jews man-made law and human authority were always suspect. They looked back on centuries of mystical experience and the only ultimate authority they recognized was that of God himself. In practical terms they longed for the establishment of a theocracy when the government should be vested in those who were steeped in the mystical tradition which they called Torah. The preliminary stage for this must be the overthrow of the 'unholy' Roman domination. Some of them even expected that God himself would intervene to bring this about.

How could the Roman officials feel safe with such a people? Sooner or later a clash was inevitable. In the meantime, while there would be no active interference with the ordinary life of the people, their activities must be closely watched and all subversive movements ruthlessly suppressed.

CHAPTER VI

AUTHORITIES FOR THE LIFE OF JESUS

BEFORE we come to consider the life of Jesus himself in this historical setting we must glance briefly at the literary sources from which our information about him derives. Not only is the material at our disposal somewhat scanty and, at least as arranged in its present form, composed a generation or more after Jesus' death, but it is also largely coloured by the beliefs of those who were already convinced of his supernatural character. There are, to be sure, scattered references to him in Jewish and Roman literature, but these are of the barest kind and tell us nothing about his life and character.

The earliest references to Jesus which we possess in literature are to be found in the Epistles of Paul some of which, e.g. to the Romans and Corinthians, must have been written in the middle years of the first century, twenty years or so after Jesus' death. Their author (originally Saul) was a Hellenized Jew who was born at Tarsus in Asia Minor. He came to Jerusalem to study in the rabbinic school under Gamaliel and in his youth was one of those who persecuted the new Christian sect. During a journey to Damascus, however, a year or two after the crucifixion, he became himself converted to the new faith through a vision (see Acts ix), with results of incalculable significance for the whole future of the Christian movement. For he set himself the task of expounding the life and death of Jesus as a regenerative force in the affairs of men, using in many of his utterances the mystical and transcendental language with which the Gentile world was already familiar through the Greek and Oriental mystery cults. He therefore embarked on a series of journeys throughout the Roman Empire and sent a number of letters to the scattered Jewish and recently formed Christian communities urging them in tender, pleading, sometimes passionate tones to live in the light of the new doctrine of salvation through belief in the risen Christ.

It is unfortunate but not surprising that these epistles throw little light on the events of Jesus' life and ministry. Paul, who did not meet Jesus himself but associated frequently with his disciples, particularly his brother James and Peter, the acknowledged leader of the Jewish-Christian Church that sprang up after Jesus' death, would assume that the story of his earthly pilgrimage was well known. He does, indeed, quote a number of his sayings or Logia, but he is chiefly interested in establishing beyond question the divine nature and redemptive power of the 'Son of God'. In these early years, moreover, it was expected that the Christ himself would soon return to earth and bring to man the promised 'kingdom'. It was only when this expectation was unrealized, and a certain scepticism about the whole doctrine began to grow up, that it was found necessary to write down and circulate some consecutive account of the life and career of the great teacher whose personality a generation earlier had set the whole Christian process in motion. The need was supplied by three writers who wove the earlier collections of Logia into a continuous narrative. This formed the substance of the first three books of the New Testament, and it is from this Gospel story (or 'good news') that we get the clearest picture of the life and teachings of the historical Jesus.

But it must be borne in mind that the Gospel writers, like the compilers of the so-called historical books of the Old Testament, were primarily interested not in history as a mere record of events, but in the significance of those events in the light of their belief in God:

> Forasmuch as many have taken in hand to draw up a narrative concerning those matters which have been fulfilled among us, even as they delivered them unto us, which from the beginning were eye-witnesses and ministers of the word, it seemed good to me also, having traced the course of all things accurately from the first, to write unto thee in order, most excellent Theophilus; that thou mightest know the certainty concerning the things wherein thou wast instructed.
>
> Luke i. 1-4.

> This is the disciple which beareth witness of these things, and wrote these things: and we know that his witness is true. And there are also many other things which Jesus did, the which if they should be written every one, I suppose that even the world itself would not contain the books that should be written.
>
> John xxi. 24-25.

The story of the life and death of Jesus was thus retold many years after his death for doctrinal purposes by those who had long made up their minds that they represented a fresh revelation from God, a unique intervention on his part in the affairs of man. Moreover, this revelation was regarded as the fulfilment of Old Testament prophecies. We should not expect from it, therefore, a dispassionate or scientific historical analysis. We need not be surprised that the Gospel writers' accounts differ in many details and that the material gives the impression of being artificially adapted to suit the requirements of Old Testament oracle. The surprising thing is, rather, that in spite of this the events of Jesus' life and his sayings were so faithfully transmitted that we are able to reconstruct an adequate history of the man from the records of religious writers compiled a considerable time after his death.

The earliest of the Gospel writers was Mark, who probably wrote for a Roman audience somewhere about the year A.D. 65. His story is the simplest, the most spontaneous, of the three. It is so homely and graphic in its presentation that it seems to reflect the observation of an eye-witness. According to Clement of Alexandria, writing about A.D. 180, 'as Peter preached the word publicly at Rome . . . many who were present requested that Mark, who had followed him for a long time and remembered his sayings, should write them out'. This, no doubt, refers to John Mark (Acts xii. 12) to whom the Gospel writer attached himself. Thus we have in Mark the most reliable account of Jesus' life, because it was nearest in point of time and in all probability records the personal impressions of Peter, his leading disciple.

Mark, together with Matthew and Luke, who probably composed their Gospels towards the end of the first century and after the fall of Jerusalem (A.D. 70), are generally described by the word 'synoptic', that is, 'having a common outlook'. This is to differentiate them from John who, as we shall see later, treated his material from a specialized, philosophic point of view and is therefore, historically speaking, less reliable. All three Synoptists, but especially Matthew and Luke, seem to have drawn from an earlier document (called by scholars Q – Quelle, source). This accounts for many similarities in language between them as does the further fact that the two later writers borrowed freely from Mark. But each has his own individual characteristics both of style and emphasis.

It is possible, and I mention this only because of my colleague's tendency to put all or most of the New Testament writings at 'a late date', that the Synoptists also made use of very early collections of some of the sayings of Jesus which some scholars believe antedated even Q.

W.W.S.

Matthew rearranged the Marcan material according to subject matter. He seems to have written for Jewish rather than Gentile Christians, in a city where the Christian population was largely Jewish in origin. He is at great pains, therefore, to relate the events of Jesus' life to Old Testament prophecy, and is particularly interested in his attitude towards the Law. There is a greater opposition to the Jews in this book than in the others, no doubt because it was written at a time when there was a growing antipathy between Synagogue and Church. It is certain that the author was not the Apostle Matthew (the publican of Matt. x. 3), but many scholars follow Papias, a Christian writer in the first half of the second century, in thinking that he incorporated in his work a Greek translation of the earlier Matthew's collected Logia, or sayings, of Jesus originally written in Aramaic. Whether this is true or not the book contains, in the Sermon on the Mount, the most complete expression of his master's ethical and social teaching.

We know a good deal more of Luke, the last of the three synoptic writers. He was also the author of the 'Acts' of the Apostles after Jesus' death and a companion of Paul, accompanying him on some of his journeys. 'Only Luke is with me', Paul writes in the Second Epistle to Timothy (iv. 11). He was a Gentile who wrote for some Greek Gentile community. He seems to have been in Jerusalem several times during his life. He thus had ample opportunities of meeting those who had known Jesus, and at Caesarea he actually lodged at the house of Philip the Evangelist. In the preface to his Gospel he writes that many had already set out to tell this story, and he incorporates a good deal of Q and Mark, but almost a third of the book (ix. 1–xviii. 14), the Peraean section as it is called, bears the stamp of his own authentic genius. He has the beautiful style of a Greek scholar and alone among the three Synoptists some genuine feeling for historical perspective.

The fourth Gospel, that of John, was probably written in the early half of the second century A.D. (or, as some scholars think, late in the first) at Ephesus in Asia Minor by a leader of the Ephesian Church. There is a tradition that he received his material direct from John, 'the beloved disciple'. The whole tone of the book suggests that at the time he wrote the Christian Church had completely severed itself from traditional Judaism and his hostility to the Jews as such is far more marked than that of the Synoptists. In places where the Synoptists refer to this or that party the writer of the fourth Gospel more often than not uses the general term 'the Jews'. The whole perspective has changed and we are in an age remote from that in which the historical Jesus lived.

There is another important consideration to be borne in mind when reading the fourth Gospel. Although some of the material is undoubtedly authentic – there are indeed reasons for believing that in some respects John is nearer to the facts than the Synoptists, especially in relation to the chronology of the closing period of the ministry of Jesus – the author's main concern was with interpretation, rather than with biography as we think of it today. He was something of a mystic, and seems to have been considerably influenced by Philo (see p. 37). This is particularly apparent in the prologue to his Gospel where his references to Jesus as 'the Word' suggests an affinity with Philo's Logos doctrine. Speaking generally, therefore, the value of his book is theological rather than historical, and for the main record of Jesus' life we have to rely on the earlier accounts in the Synoptic Gospels.

These can only be very thinly supplemented, as has been already made clear, by contemporary (or subsequent) Roman and Jewish literature. Indeed, the references to Jesus made by Roman authors add nothing to our knowledge either of his life or his teaching; but we should scarcely expect the Roman world to be interested in yet another religious belief. The historian Tacitus (A.D. 115) does, however, mention the Christians as being blamed by Nero for setting fire to Rome in A.D. 64, and he adds: 'This name comes from Christ, whom the Procurator Pontius Pilate, under the rule of Tiberius, had handed over to torture.' There is also Pliny's famous letter to Trajan, written about A.D. 112, when as governor in Bithynia he asks for advice in dealing with the new sect who sing hymns to 'one Christus, a God'. Finally there is a possible reference to Jesus in Suetonius' life of the Emperor Claudius who, he says, 'banished from Rome the Jews who made a great tumult because of Christus'.

The references in Jewish literature are more numerous but scarcely more illuminating. The oldest come in Josephus, who was born in Jerusalem a few years after Jesus' death. Some scholars have suspected their genuineness but, though expanded by a later writer, they probably have an authentic core. The first (*Antiquities*, 18. 3, iii) tells us that Jesus came into prominence about the time of the rising against Pilate caused by his attempt to use the Temple revenues to improve Jerusalem's water supply (see p. 61). It refers to him as 'a wise man' and 'a doer of wonderful works'. It goes on to say that 'he drew over to him many of the Jews and many of the Gentiles . . . and when Pilate at the suggestion of the principal men among us had condemned him to the cross, those that loved him at the first ceased not to do so . . . and the race of Christians, so named from him, are not extinct even now'. In the second passage (*Antiquities*, 20. 9, i) Jesus is mentioned so casually that its genuineness need not be doubted. It runs as follows: 'Ananias called a Sanhedrin together, brought before it James the brother of Jesus, who was called the Christ, and certain others whom he regarded as breakers of the Law, and condemned them to be stoned.'

There are a fair number of references to Jesus scattered about Talmud and Midrash (rabbinic interpretation, commentary on the scriptures). None was written before the fall of Jerusalem and, as we should expect, they nearly all reflect the growing hostility of the Jewish people towards the new Christian sect. Their prejudiced and tendentious character thus renders them almost useless as sources of information about Jesus' life.

Nevertheless a distinction can be drawn between the earlier passages of what is called the Tannaitic period (*Tannaim*: composers of the Mishnah in the first and second centuries A.D.) and those written after Hadrian's persecutions and right on into the time of the *Amoraim* (compilers of the *Gemarah*) in the third and fourth centuries. The earlier and more reliable ones show much less hostility to Jesus and his teaching than the later ones which were probably the product of Jewish persecution at Christian hands. They describe Jesus (Yeshu of Nazareth) as a true Jew, though 'an Israelite who had sinned'. His rank is higher than that of 'the prophets of the Gentiles', and he is assured of a share in the world to come. He is even regarded as one of the scribes and Tannaim, and one of his expositions pleased so severe a critic as

Rabbi Eliezer the Great (born about A.D. 30 or 40). Yet he practised sorcery and healed the diseased by magic. He expounded scripture like the Pharisees but 'made a mock of the words of the wise'. He said that he was not come to take anything away from the Law nor to add to it, yet he beguiled and led Israel astray. He was about thirty-three years old when he was executed as a false teacher 'on the eve of Passover, which happened on a Sabbath'.

These statements have the authentic ring of early rabbinic opposition to the new heresy and its founder. They are mildness itself compared with the wild extravagances of later Talmudic writings. Here we find the bitterest antipathy to Jesus and the Minim (heretics) as, according to some scholars, his followers were called. All sorts of stories are told about his birth. He was alleged to be the illegitimate son of an adulteress. His father was said by some to be a Roman soldier called Pandera or Pantera. Some scholars have connected this name with the Greek 'Parthenos', maiden or virgin. He is accused of 'making himself God'. There is a story that when he was to be put to death a herald was despatched to announce the fact forty days before the date was fixed for his execution so that anyone might come forward and plead his cause. No one could be found to do so. Doubts, even, were raised as to whether such a man would have any share in the world to come.

All this apocryphal, jaundiced material was later collected and finally published in a book called *Tol'doth Yeshu*, or 'The Generations of Jesus'. The date of this is uncertain though it was probably not earlier than the tenth century. The book has no historical value, for it was written to discredit Christianity and its founder and its inventions and legends do nothing but heap upon him ridicule and abuse. It is only important, therefore, as showing the fearful deterioration which had taken place in Jewish-Christian relations after the first century and how easily men's judgment may become warped and distorted through persecution. Only recently has it become possible for Christian and Jew to shake off this traditional habit of mutual suspicion and recrimination, to penetrate these early mists of false legend and misrepresentation which seemed to have settled on their minds for ever, and to see each other clearly for what they are – brothers in spirit.

If only there had been a contemporary biography of Jesus, such as Tacitus' Life of Agricola, written either by a Roman or a Jew, interested in him from a more detached standpoint than that of the four evangelists, a great deal of this misconception with its tragic consequences might never have arisen. But that was not to be, for detachment seems not to have been easily achieved in matters relating to Jesus of Nazareth.

Fortunately, however, the Gospel writers have left us a fair amount of material from which a reasonably accurate portrait can be painted. But it must be remembered that their interest was focused only on the years of his ministry, and those years, for them, were full of mystery and wonder which inevitably coloured their records. We therefore know nothing, or next to nothing, of the whole of the first thirty years of his life. Indeed, interest in the childhood and youth of great men is a comparatively recent development. The void can only be filled in by a judicious use of the imagination, by recourse to the probable or plausible, judged from the known facts of the historical background. This is always a dangerous expedient, for it gives far too large a scope for the subjective element so often found in the writing of history. Nevertheless, there is no other way of 'piercing behind the early interpretations', of recovering the Jesus of history, and painting as accurate and sensitive a portrait as the circumstances allow.

CHAPTER VII

JESUS' CHILDHOOD AND EARLY MINISTRY

THE birth of the first male child was from very early times an event of special importance in Jewish families. There was not only the 'Berith Milah' (circumcision) ceremony to be performed on the eighth day in the case of all male children, but also the Redemption of the Firstborn on the thirtieth. This custom is said to have originated from the fact that Hebrew children were spared the tenth plague when all the firstborn of Egypt were slain by the angel of death. They were, therefore, especially consecrated to God and the father marked the occasion by a payment of five shekels to the priest and the holding of a special feast.

We may be sure that when Jesus was born the customary ritual was observed. His parents, Joseph, a carpenter of Nazareth, and Mary, were of pure Israelitish stock. His original name was therefore Joshua ben (the son of) Joseph, Jesus being the Greek form of Joshua. They were simple Galilean folk of the artisan class, struggling hard, it may be presumed, in that age of poverty and exploitation to earn a precarious livelihood. In course of time they had a large family (by modern standards), consisting probably of five boys and two or three girls. This we gather from a passage in Mark vi. 3: 'Is not this the carpenter, the son of Mary, and brother of James, and Joses, and Judas, and Simon? and are not his sisters here with us?' The father, Joseph, may be presumed to have died when they were young, for we hear nothing further of him when reference is made to the rest of the family.

The little town in which they lived, Nazareth, lay on the slope of a green hill in southern Galilee from whose summit there was a magnificent view of the adjacent country. To the south could be seen the hills of Samaria beyond the plain of Esdraelon, to the west the Mediterranean seaboard stretching northwards in the direction of Tyre and Mount Hermon, to the east the Jordan valley and the high hills of Bashan. Below and around the town were fields of wheat and barley, high-growing but thin-eared, and forests of palm, fig-tree and pomegranate are still to be seen there. It was a peaceful place, cut off from the busy world and the main caravan routes, living on its own country produce and handicrafts. Its inhabitants were poor, despised folk, typical Am-ha-aretz of whom it was said, 'Can any good thing come out of Nazareth?' (John i. 46). But a few miles to the north and within walking distance lay the important town of Sepphoris, rebuilt in the Greek style during Jesus' boyhood. Through this passed the great high road from the coast to Tiberias (founded by Herod Antipas and named in honour of Tiberius) and Damascus. To the north-east was the sea of Galilee, famous for its fishing industry, and beyond this again Lake Merom, surrounded by forest and jungle, where Herod and his court hunted panther, leopards, bears, foxes and other wild game.

We can imagine the carpenter's young family playing and wandering about these fields round Nazareth, watching the corn ripen and the harvest being cut, learning the names of trees and flowers and birds as country children do. The language of Jesus in later life bore traces of this early contact with nature, and sheep, cows, asses, sparrows, flowers, and the bright sun were the familiar objects of his talk. In this he resembled Amos, the herdsman of Tekoa, and his own great forerunner, Jeremiah. He was an imaginative and, perhaps, in a sense lonely boy, and he must often have wandered on the hill above his village to see the great world passing at a leisurely camel's pace along the high road to east and west. For the main interest in his life was always man, man in all the variety and complexity of his nature, man, too, in the simplest and most comprehensive terms, as a child of the living God.

Much of his time must have been spent helping his mother at home and learning, and later practising, his craft in the carpenter's shop. He became a great story-teller and the background of his home – the heating of ovens, the leavening of bread, clothes with their patches, candles, bushels, beds, rust and the rest – set the tone to much of his conversation. He must have been an exceptionally observant child and a good deal given to abstraction of thought. It is scarcely likely that his family understood him; at one point in his life they clearly thought him bewitched. 'And when his friends heard it, they went out to lay hold on him: for they said, He is beside himself' (Mark iii. 21). Perhaps in some ways he was a difficult child to bring up, liable to question authority and capable of sudden fits of wilfulness and temper.

When I first read this reference to 'sudden fits of wilfulness and temper' my instinctive reaction was, first, to protest strongly and, secondly, to suggest the omission of the words. On second thoughts, rightly or wrongly, I decided that to urge my own point of view too strongly would be to do an injustice to the integrity of my friend's approach to our subject. What we have here is a sketch for a portrait of Jesus as he appears to a non-Christian reader of the New Testament story. It is hardly surprising that he should see and feel differently from the Christian who has been brought up to take so much, perhaps even too much, for granted. Perhaps, after all, it will do our Christian readers no more harm than it has done me to find myself shaken out of a certain complacency and faced with the necessity of trying to see through another's eyes things which, by reason of their very familiarity, I have almost ceased to see through my own. I have made this point here because, as the reader will quickly realize, if he has not done so already, it applies equally well to other details both in this and in the following chapters.   W.W.S.

There is the story of his disappearance as a boy of twelve, told by Luke (ii. 41–51) which, though possibly a legend, nevertheless illustrates the sort of impression he made on his contemporaries. The family were making one of their pilgrimages to Jerusalem at the festival of Passover and on the return journey noticed that Jesus was missing from the caravan. They returned to Jerusalem in search of him and found him in the Temple sitting and disputing with the Doctors, who were 'amazed at his understanding and his answers'. His parents upbraided him for his lack of consideration to themselves. Whereupon came the quick retort: 'How is it that ye sought me? wist ye not that I must be in my Father's house?' Truly a difficult and precocious child. Yet his kindliness, serious ways, and deep sympathy for all those who were in distress must have won him many lasting friends among his contemporaries. We can imagine especially how his younger brothers and sisters ran to him for comfort and consolation when they were in trouble, how he became the natural leader of children, someone whom they could trust, whose incomparable talk and stories fascinated, yet puzzled, them and kept them from work and play.

Religious observance and ceremonial were, as we have seen, an inseparable part of the life of a Jewish child, and we may be sure that Jesus was strictly brought up on the principles of the Torah. This means that he would be taken to the Synagogue as soon as he could walk and that he early learned to read the most familiar passages from the scriptures (such as the Shema) in Hebrew and to take part in all the religious ceremonial of the home. From infancy the beautiful and picturesque symbolism would have aroused his eager curiosity. There were the *mezuzah* on the door-post, the *tephillin* (phylacteries) worn by his father, the sanctification (*Kiddush*) over bread and wine prior to the Sabbath meal, the ritual washing of the hands, the booth which the family inhabited for a week in the autumn at the festival of Tabernacles (*Succoth*), and all the elaborate ceremonial of the Passover Night service, from time immemorial the Jewish child's 'Christmas Eve'. All this and much more the growing boy would absorb, learning to cherish, not perhaps without discrimination, the customs of his ancestors.

At the age of thirteen, presumably he became 'Barmitzvah' (confirmed) and in accordance with tradition recited a passage from the Hebrew scripture in the local synagogue. But we have no authentic record of Jesus' life until he came under the influence of John the Baptist, who began to preach in the fifteenth year of the Emperor Tiberius (A.D. 29). There is some discrepancy about dates, but according to Luke Jesus was then thirty years old, and we must picture him during all this earlier time as having to work hard at the carpenter's shop in Nazareth in order to support his large family after their father's death. Yet the young man's life must have been filled with other things as well. This was the period when he studied and got to love the ancient scriptures, learned passages of the Torah, the Psalms and the Prophets by heart, and took an active part in the teaching and ceremonial of the local synagogue. There would be time, too, for roaming across the Galilean hills, watching the sheep grazing, the lilies growing in the field, the yearly golden miracle of the harvests; more distant excursions, perhaps, to the lake where he would become familiar with the fishing industry and get to know the ways of the simple fishing folk and their homely talk. But always there would be the man apart, the wistful, tender yet passionate nature, the penetrating intelligence, brooding on the mystery behind mortal life, waiting for the right moment to express itself, to reveal the secrets slowly learned of a God-created world.

It was inevitable that such a man should come under the influence of the fiery Jewish preacher who was at this time drawing large numbers to the wilderness round Jericho. His Hebrew name was probably Jochanan ben Zachariah, the priest, but throughout the ages he has been called John the Baptist, owing to the importance he attached to ritual cleansing by immersion in the waters of Jordan. This practice he may have learned from the Essenes, but he does not seem to have belonged to any of their exclusive guilds, for he did not urge men to forsake their normal occupations and go out into the wilderness. His message was universal and, like the apocalyptic Pharisees, he was consumed with a passionate belief that the end of the world was at hand and that man must repent from his sins before it was too late.

It is possible that he thought of himself as the Prophet Elijah reborn, who was to announce the coming of the Messiah. In any case, dressing in wild attire, he denounced the wickedness of Antipas, the Roman tetrarch, especially for his marriage with his brother's wife, Herodias, contrary to the Law of Moses, just as the earlier Prophet had hurled his bitterest invective against Ahab, the King of Israel, and his Phoenician wife, Jezebel, who attempted to introduce an alien cult among the people of the Lord. Antipas was more successful than his prototype in crushing opposition, and he caused John to be arrested and shut up in the fortress of Machaerus. Finally he put him to death, probably at the suggestion of his wife Herodias, as a political agitator who was inciting the people to revolt. There is also the Gospel story, which has a distinctly legendary flavour, that Antipas held a birthday feast at which Salome, the daughter of Herodias, danced and 'pleased Herod and them that sat at meat with him'. He promised to give her whatever she wanted and, after consulting her mother, she asked 'that thou forthwith give me in a charger the head of John the Baptist'. The King, though 'exceeding sorry', stuck to his oath and gave orders for John's immediate execution (see Mark vi. 17–29). It is significant that Josephus does not mention this story. What he does say, however, in describing the defeat of Antipas some years later at the hands of Aretas IV, King of Arabia, is that 'many Jews saw in the destruction of Herod's army a just punishment from God for the killing of John who was called the Baptist'.

The baptism of Jesus by John proved a turning point in the young man's career. The passive role became a thing of the past, and he began to see more clearly the shape of things to come and the active part he was destined to play. First he retired for a brief period into the wilderness to ponder and pray, perhaps to prepare his mind for some irrevocable decision. Here we may imagine he laid bare once more before himself and before his Maker all those troubled and tempestuous thoughts that had raged in his brain ever since he was a little boy in the Galilean home. He had been taught to love God with all his heart, soul and might. How could he best show that love? Why was there so much sin and suffering in the world, and why did God's creatures behave so callously and inhumanly to one another? What was the point of the endless religious observances and ceremonial when those who scrupulously obeyed the enactments of the Law so often forgot to be loving and merciful in their daily lives?

His contact with John and the experience of baptism must have set other thoughts in motion as well. We have already seen how the Jewish people of the age into which Jesus was born were, in their oppressed and helpless condition, lifting expectant eyes on high and looking for some sign of divine deliverance. John, with his obsession about Elijah the Prophet (based on Malachi iv. 5), announced that he had come to proclaim the kingdom of heaven and the advent of the Messiah. This may have confirmed certain shadowy, half-formulated imaginings in Jesus' own mind. Might he himself not be the one chosen to show men the ways of God, to deliver them from the tyranny of evil, to usher in the reign of peace and goodwill on earth? This would account for the peculiar feeling of intimacy, the intensity and passion of the love he had always felt for his heavenly Father in the secret places of his heart.

At about this time, then, Jesus may have begun to think of himself as the Messiah, the anointed servant sent by God to deliver mankind, and this bold self-identification seems to have coloured the whole of his subsequent ministry. But first he had to make up his mind what kind of role Messiahship should take. We have seen how the Jewish people at this time were divided in their conception of the nature of the intervention which all alike so confidently expected. To some it seemed that there would arise a human deliverer, possibly a child of the house of David, who would free Israel from the oppressor's yoke and make her a leader of the nations. All peoples would then flock to Jerusalem to hear the word of the Lord, and an age of peace and prosperity would be ushered in both for Israel and for the rest of the world. The second, or apocalyptic, view was that miraculously there would descend from heaven 'the Son of Man', a divine agent who would bring the old world order to an end and proclaim the advent of the kingdom of God.

Jesus, who was well versed in both the prophetic writings and the eschatological teachings of the so-called Daniel literature (see pp. 38-9), must have pondered on these Messianic conceptions for many a long year during his youth and early manhood. But for the practical purposes of everyday life there was another side of Jewish teaching that had profoundly influenced him. He had been brought up in the Pharisaic tradition and much of his interest centred on the Synagogue and the practice of Torah. He was able to expound and discourse on points of law like the learned scholars, and it was as a Rabbi or teacher of more than usual originality that he was first known among the simple people of Nazareth.

In making his great decision in the wilderness, it is possible that Jesus purposely refrained from defining the nature of his future ministry in exact terms, that he even hovered between two or more conceptions of the Messianic role and determined to let events shape, to some extent, his future course. What is certain is that he made some final rejections. He would emphatically refuse to play the part of a Zealot leader (though this might have secured him a large following in Galilee) and take militant action against Roman authority. Nor would his function henceforth be confined by the legalism and hair-splitting which characterized much of the rabbinic method of approach. The Messiah must be a free lance, untrammelled by orthodox teaching or conventional morality. He was responsible only to the Father in heaven who had sent him to bring salvation to his erring and suffering children. And they were in desperate need for, as he had heard from John the Baptist and believed with all the ardour of an unquestioning faith, the day of the Lord was at hand and only the righteous would share in the heavenly kingdom that was to follow.

The whole of this internal struggle in the mind of Jesus is described in the beautiful allegorical story of the Gospel known as 'The Temptation'. It seems clear from it that, if he had ever dreamed of Messiahship in terms of worldly power or that spurious but short-lived reputation that may be gained from a sensational application of magic, he now put both these firmly out of his mind.

And the devil said unto him, If thou art the Son of God, command this stone that it become bread. And Jesus answered unto him, It is written, Man shall not live by bread alone. And he led him up, and shewed him all the kingdoms of the world in a moment of time. And the devil said unto him, To thee will I give all this authority, and the glory of them: for it hath been delivered unto me; and to whomsoever I will I give it. If thou therefore wilt worship before me, it shall all be thine. And Jesus answered and said unto him, It is written, Thou shalt worship the Lord thy God, and him only shalt thou serve. And he led him to Jerusalem, and set him on the pinnacle of the temple, and said unto him, If thou art the Son of God, cast thyself down from hence: for it is written,

He shall give his angels charge concerning thee, to guard thee:
and,
    On their hands they shall bear thee up,
    Lest haply thou dash thy foot against a stone.

And Jesus answering said unto him, It is said, Thou shalt not tempt the Lord thy God. And when the devil had completed every temptation, he departed from him for a season.

Luke iv. 3–13.

After this for a time Jesus seems to have gone back to Nazareth and to his normal life there, but always now with the expectation of some call to fresh action. Soon came the news that John the Baptist had been arrested, and this event was to him the dread summons to a wholly new way of life. He must step into the great preacher's shoes, proclaim the gospel of the kingdom of heaven and call on men to repent while there was yet time. Only in one thing would his message differ from that of his 'forerunner'. It must be made plain that the days were already fulfilled and that the longed-for Messiah had come. But for the present he would keep his identity a close secret.

At this point he turned his back on the carpenter's shop at Nazareth for ever and became an itinerant preacher in the towns and villages of Galilee. To help him in his task he began to collect a small band of followers, the first of whom were all fishermen on the Galilean lake: Simon and Andrew, whom he promised to make 'fishers of men', and James and John, the sons of Zebedee. He had already learnt the secret of the delegation of responsibility – that if a great regenerative movement is to succeed it must depend not only on the leadership of a single individual, but on his capacity to inspire a small band of devoted followers. His first public appearance since the departure from Nazareth was at Capernaum, a fishing town on the banks of the lake which, before the foundation of Tiberias (about A.D. 16), had been the most important centre of commerce in Galilee. He chose this as the scene of his activity also because his first disciple, Simon (later called Peter, or 'the rock') lived there with his wife's mother, and she warmly received him as a guest. To begin with, he played the part of an ordinary Pharisaic Rabbi, but with a difference. He preached in the Synagogue, expounding the Law and the Prophets, but his audiences were immediately struck with something new and unfamiliar in his method. He spoke 'as one that had authority'. This means that he did not confine himself to quoting the opinions of scholars and legal experts (like the Scribes) and delivering a balanced judgment as between them. His approach resembled that of the Prophets of old who prefaced their 'oracles' by the formula 'thus saith the Lord'. But he took full personal responsibility for his teachings, using the phrase, 'But I say unto you '. So that, more than in the case of most contemporary Rabbis, his words bore the impress of his own special personality.

Another special feature of his teaching was a bold use of parable and allegory. The Tannaim also employed the allegorical method in exposition, but less frequently than the scriptural. Jesus nearly always expressed or illustrated his ethical and moral judgments by means of a parable, and this for two reasons. First, he was addressing simple peasants or fisher-folk – the Am-ha-aretz – who would more readily understand and appreciate his teaching if it was couched in homely language. 'Unto you [the disciples] is given the mystery of the kingdom of God: but unto them that are without, all things are done in parables' (Mark iv. 11–12). Secondly, he had a genius for telling stories and his lively imagination would find the parable form best suited to express his keen sense of the 'poetry of life'. For there is this baffling or haunting quality of the parable, that while it treats of the everyday things of common experience, it sets the mind questioning and speculating about their inner mystery.

Yes ... but! With all that A.I.P. says about the parables I agree. It is what he does not say that makes me want to add this note, for his quotation from St. Mark stops short at a very significant and difficult point. For the evangelist represents Jesus as going on to say (and here he is quoting from Isaiah vi. 9–10) that the reason for talking to 'them that are without' – a suggestive phrase, that! – in parables is 'that seeing they may see, and not perceive; and hearing they may hear, and not understand; lest haply they should turn again, and it should be forgiven them'. I venture to complete the quotation, not because I think it makes the story any easier to understand, but rather because it serves to emphasize what I have felt for a long time to be the case, that there is more to the parables than meets the eye.

On the lips of Jesus at any rate they are part of the mystery of the Kingdom of God and of his own function in relation to the coming of that Kingdom. If they were as simple and straightforward as we are sometimes encouraged to believe, it is difficult to understand why the Kingdom is so long in coming. Perhaps, after all, the frequent admonition of one of my own schoolmasters – and he, too, was quoting scripture, this time Jeremiah – has some bearing on this also: 'O foolish people, and without understanding; which have eyes and see not; which have ears and hear not.' Polack is surely right when he insists that the parable 'sets the mind questioning and speculating'. But the question is – about what?   W.W.S.

A third characteristic of Jesus' early ministry was his healirg of the sick. This gift, even more than his preaching, seems at first to have been responsible for attracting the big crowds by which he was invariably followed. It is difficult to know in precise terms what this particular skill involved. Medical science had not advanced as far in Palestine at that time as in Greece or Rome under the influence of the Hippocratic schools though, no doubt, the Greek and Roman conquerors and administrators had professional doctors among their entourage. There is no evidence that Jesus, like Luke, had any specific medical training, but his studies in Torah and the discourses of the rabbinic schools would often turn on questions of hygiene. From ancient times the Prophets (e.g. Elisha) and the religious teachers were regarded as being possessed of healing powers, and the wonder-Rabbi was as common a type among the ancient Jews as among Chassidic Jews today, or as the fakir in modern India.

We have seen that Jesus moved about among credulous, unsophisticated folk, and they clearly regarded his cures as miraculous. But the probability is that his strong faith enabled him to impart faith to others and that he was possessed of unusual psychic and hypnotic powers. At this time in Palestine, and particularly in Galilee, a long period of war and oppression had left in its wake the usual heavy toll of suffering and depression, with its attendant evils of neurosis and physical paralysis. People who suffered these mental and functional disorders were often regarded in ancient times as possessed by a demon or evil spirit, and we read in such stories as those of Saul and Nebuchadnezzar how derangement of mind could lead to a total loss of energy and will. Jesus had just the right personality to minister to such 'lost souls' and restore their confidence and mental health. Thus his success in 'driving out devils' or exorcising the evil spirit gained him a great reputation among the simple Galileans, but he seems to have been reluctant to make full use of his powers. This may be accounted for in two ways. The exercise of hypnotic suggestion, the superimposition of one will on another, is a great physical strain, and probably led in each case to temporary exhaustion. Jesus knew the limitations of his power, and was always afraid that his message would be misunderstood and irrelevant demands made on him. Moreover, he felt that his real function in life was not that of a physician in the ordinary sense but a curer of souls. There was always a risk that he would be followed for the wrong reasons.

As with the parables, so also in the case of the miracles I cannot help feeling that we are in the presence of something even more mysterious than is implied by the suggestion that Jesus 'was possessed of unusual psychic and hypnotic powers'. If we are to judge by St. Mark's account, the questions to which both the miracles and the parables gave rise in the minds of those who heard or saw them were not: 'What does he mean?' or 'How does he do these things?' but 'Who is this?' And if we are to judge by another of St. Mark's stories, where he tells how Jesus himself put this very question to his disciples at Caesarea Philippi, on an occasion which proved to be the turning-point in his ministry, the moral seems to be that in the very moment in which we are reasonably confident that we know the right answer we are as likely as not to discover that we are as far as ever from understanding what it really means. For Peter, who in one moment made what many might have thought to be his supreme profession of faith, found himself rebuked in the next for 'minding not the things of God, but the things of men' (Mark viii. 27 ff). W.W.S.

The great publicity aroused by his teaching and 'miraculous' healings caused him to leave Capernaum for a time and shake off the crowds who now began to follow him about. No doubt his sensitive soul still suffered from diffidence, still felt an inner shrinking from the full implications of a task which brooked no denial, and he required a further period of seclusion and self-examination. Perhaps, too, the awful fate of John the Baptist hovered before his eyes. His disciples tried to bring him back, but he preferred to wander about the villages of Galilee and deliver his message in a more subdued light.

After a time he returned to his headquarters at Capernaum and one of his first acts was to visit the house of a customs official or publican, Levi (or Mattathiah) ben Halphai (Alphaeus), the Matthew in the Gospel account who subsequently became one of his disciples. Here he consorted with Matthew's friends, 'publicans and sinners', as they were described in the current jargon. This conduct started his estrangement from the stricter Pharisees, who were deeply shocked at the sight of the 'wonder-Rabbi' sitting down at table with the dregs of the populace. There is a good modern parallel in the attitude of official Hinduism to Gandhi when he espoused the cause of the Untouchables.

From now onwards Jesus took every opportunity of asserting his deep feeling for humanity, his belief in fundamental moral principle even when this clashed with conventional practice. He absolved his disciples from fasting since they are 'sons of the bride-chamber' attending the bridegroom himself – a reference to the joyful coming of the Messiah.[1] He championed the cause of the simple fisher-folk, the Am-ha-aretz, of whom even the gentle Hillel observed that 'no Am-ha-aretz can be a pious man'. Once he told a paralysed man that his sins were forgiven, a statement which the Pharisees regarded as blasphemous; for 'who can forgive sins but God alone?'[2] He allowed ears of corn to be plucked on the sabbath to satisfy hunger. More serious still, he cured a cripple on the sabbath though his life was not in danger, on the principle, which had sound rabbinic support, that 'the sabbath was made for man, and not man for the sabbath'.

All this roused the hostility of the local Pharisees, who began to resort to open action against him. They did this in two ways. They

[1] Matt. ix. 15.
[2] Luke v. 21.

sent a deputation to Tiberias, Herod's capital, to instigate Herod's officials and the local magistrates to arrest him; and they tried to alienate his own followers among the people by saying that he was a friend of transgressors and that his cures were due to the possession of unholy powers derived from Beelzebub, the prince of devils. Even his mother and brothers were converted to this view and sought to restrain him from further eccentricity. They seem to have been alarmed about his mental condition and tried to bring him back to the family life at Nazareth. There may have been a further motive for their action. Since his father's death Jesus had been the head of the family and the mainstay of their support. Now that he had gone the carpenter's shop lacked its chief craftsman and the family, no doubt, were faced with the prospect of increasing poverty.

Jesus was quite uncompromising in the face of these attempts to bring him to reason. All the answers to his critics show that his mind was made up and that he was inexorably committed to the task he had set himself. If he consorts with transgressors it is because the sick need healing, not the whole. His mother and family have no special claim on him; 'for whosoever shall do the will of God, the same is my brother, and sister, and mother' (Mark iii. 35).

Yet he was conscious of the danger to which this line of conduct exposed him. For a time he gave up teaching by the seashore. He took a boat out on the sea itself and spoke to his followers from a distance, or sometimes they gathered about him in a string of boats. This not only enabled him to avoid the pressure of the crowd but also made capture by Herod's officers more difficult. Alternatively, he retired away from towns and gathered his followers, not so numerous as they were, in some remote and secluded spot. It was at this time that he felt a sudden desire to revisit the haunts of his youth. He returned to Nazareth and preached once more in the local synagogue. But here he seems to have had little success with his 'faith cures' and to have aroused expectations which he could not fulfil. It is a common experience that doctors and preachers are not at their best with their own families, since familiarity is apt to breed distrust and set up unconscious barriers of resistance. In this case Jesus certainly provoked the hostility of his fellow-townsmen, and the rough treatment he received at their hands led to one of his occasional moods of depression and defeatism. 'No prophet is acceptable in his own country', he exclaims. He never saw Nazareth again.

Perhaps it was his experience at Nazareth and the comparative failure of his mission hitherto that led him to review his technique, for he seems, about this time, to have decided that his ministry must be more broadly based. We have seen that he had already gathered four disciples about him of whom Peter (Simon ben Jonah) was the chief. To them were now added Matthew, the customs officer, and seven others, the total twelve being chosen to correspond with the number of the tribes of Israel. Their names, according to Mark, were Philip, Bartholomew, Thomas, James, the son of Alphaeus, Thaddaeus, another Simon and Judas. The latter, referred to as Iscariot (Ish Kerioth, a man of Kerioth), was the only one of the twelve who came from Judaea, all the rest being Galileans. Of most of them we know very little, and it is curious that, though the task of proclaiming the teaching of Jesus after his death must have devolved upon these 'apostles', the chief founders of the early Church except for Peter, such as James, the brother of Jesus, Paul and Barnabas, were not of their number.

These twelve disciples henceforth shared the work of their master and they were sent out in pairs through the villages to preach the speedy coming of the kingdom and to urge on men the necessity of repentance and good works. They were expressly told not to go to the Gentiles or to any city of the Samaritans, for Jesus had not, so far, at any rate, shaken off his early nationalist training, and he felt that his mission was primarily to the 'lost sheep of the house of Israel' (Matt. x. 6). Only after Israel had been redeemed would the Gentiles 'be added to the house of Jacob'. Like the Essenes, the disciples were to give up all property and take no money with them on their journey. If they were not hospitably received at any place, they must shake off its dust from the soles of their feet and wander elsewhere. They must use diplomacy, even subtlety, Matthew writes, since they were 'as sheep in the midst of wolves'.

This strategy was immediately successful. The disciples gained the confidence and experience which they required, and some of their master's unique powers began to be shared by them. But the more the movement grew, the more it aroused the apprehension of Antipas who felt that his authority in Galilee, that breeding-ground of Zealots and nationalist rebels, was being threatened by one who proclaimed the coming of a new kingdom. He had got rid of one John the Baptist; he did not want his position undermined by another. Jesus became aware that it was no longer safe for him to remain in Galilee. He set sail across the sea and landed at Beth-saida, the nearest town outside the tetrarchy of Antipas, and perhaps the home of his disciple, Philip.

He did not stay long there but wandered about the valley of Gennesaret to the north. His movement was receiving widespread support—perhaps too much to please the Galilean Pharisees. It seems that they were now joined by a number of 'Pharisees and scribes from Jerusalem' (Matt. xv. 1) who had either come to Galilee by chance or were summoned by their colleagues in order to investigate the conduct of this unorthodox Rabbi. Their suspicions were at once aroused and all their old prejudices against the Am-ha-aretz confirmed. Why, they asked, did this Jewish teacher allow his disciples to neglect ceremonial obligations such as the washing of hands before meals and thus 'transgress the traditions of the elders?' Jesus, to whom a right understanding of the Law was a dominant concern, was deeply hurt. His resentment was expressed in bitter taunts and recriminations. 'Why', he asked them, 'do ye also transgress the commandment of God because of your tradition?' Instancing their abuse of the Corban, or religious offering, by making it a pretext for avoiding a man's obligation to support his parents, he asserted that their tradition had caused them to make void the word of God. Finally he turned for support to the crowd, disclosing to them his whole belief in the paramount claims of the moral law: 'Not that which entereth into the mouth defileth the man; but that which proceedeth out of the mouth, this defileth the man' (Matt- xv. 2). [1]The die was cast. This Pharisee could no longer work within the framework of rabbinic tradition. The time had come for him to reveal himself in the Messianic role and declare the secret of his mission to men.

[1] The dietary laws were an integral part of Halachah (the Rabbinic code).

CHAPTER VIII

LATER MINISTRY AND DEATH

IT is not possible to be sure about the chronological sequence of events during the remainder of Jesus' life or the length of time his ministry lasted. The best evidence seems to show that about a year elapsed between the baptism and his final breach with the Pharisees, and that the last crowded events took place within two or three months. The whole ministry, in any case, did not last more than three years and was probably confined to less than half this period. We are dealing, therefore, with a man of just over thirty years of age who, for reasons which are not by any means self-evident, was condemned to death during the reign of Tiberius, probably in A.D. 29.

The crisis described in the last chapter led Jesus to alter his whole plan of campaign. His quarrel with the Pharisees convinced him that the time had come to throw off the role of Pharisaic Rabbi and announce himself as the long-expected Messiah. But for the moment he showed signs of considerable uncertainty and apprehension. Always a deeply sensitive person, the attacks of Pharisee and Herodian, with some accompanying loss of popular support, had thrown him into a mood of bitter despondency. He left the haunts of his fellow-Jews and wandered for a time through Tyre and Sidon. Here occurred the incident of the Phoenician woman in which some instinctive feeling of national exclusiveness within him seemed suddenly to assert itself. 'It is not meet to take the children's [i.e. Israel's] bread and cast it to the dogs', he says to the mother who begs him to cure her child (Matt. xv. 26). But he is quick to repent of this impetuous outburst and with characteristic generosity accedes to her request. Here, too, in his bitterness of heart he uttered the fiercest denunciations against the Galilean towns that had refused to recognize his work and accept his teachings. And by means of the parable of the wedding guests he arraigned those elements, such as the Pharisees and Scribes, who had rejected him and reduced his following to the mere dregs of the people, the harlots, publicans and sinners who had always exerted a special appeal to his generous heart.

The attribution to Jesus of 'moods of bitter despondency' and 'bitterness of heart' will seem to many Christian readers entirely out of keeping with their understanding of his character and personality. May I therefore refer to what I have already said in my note on p. 75 and express the hope that any who feel provoked by such phrases will use the provocation as a challenge to re-examine their own hearts as they try to see through my colleague's eyes. W.W.S.

Once more he returned to the Sea of Galilee but remained on the east side, where the population was largely Gentile, and wandered through the Decapolis, or ten cities. Even here he was afraid to enter the cities themselves lest his actions should be reported, and it is some evidence of his feeling of being rejected that he was able to say to a would-be follower: 'The foxes have holes, and the birds of the heaven have nests; but the Son of man hath not where to lay his head' (Matt. viii. 20). Again he spent a short time in Galilee (the regions of Dalmanutha) but, failing or being unwilling to give a sign and fearing arrest, he crossed once more to Philip's territory. After a brief second visit to Beth-saida he journeyed farther north and arrived at 'the parts of Caesarea Philippi'.

Here occurred the second turning-point in Jesus' career. In the quiet of a remote country village, somewhere on the slopes of Hermon, he began to question his disciples as to what men thought about him. Peter's answer that he was the Christ, God's anointed servant, received his acceptance. He explained to them in precise terms the nature of his mission and outlined an immediate course of action. He must go up to Jerusalem, announce the coming of God's kingdom, be subjected to intense suffering culminating, perhaps, in his own death, but finally reign triumphant when the great intervention from on high shall have taken place and a revolution have been effected in the spirit of man. Those who followed him must likewise be prepared for suffering at the hands of their opponents and the ruling powers. For the moment they must keep their knowledge a closely guarded secret. But the time for disclosure would not be long delayed.

His disciples, particularly Peter, were aghast at this programme. They had already experienced the hostility of their fellow-

Galileans, and had seen their master in moods of dejection. Their native common sense told them what they must expect in the capital, the centre of the priesthood and Roman authority, where they would already be regarded with suspicion as ignorant country folk with a propensity for lawlessness and insurrection. Jesus had to silence their protests, but characteristically he did this less with words than by imparting to them some of his own spirit and burning conviction. Three of them, Peter, James and John, followed him to the top of Hermon, and there he seems suddenly to have appeared to them as a man transfigured. To their simple intelligence he no longer looked like the Galilean carpenter or itinerant Rabbi but like a supernatural being who was indeed the 'anointed servant' of their dreams. If they still retained some lingering doubts on account of the popular belief that the Messiah must be preceded by the coming of Elijah, Jesus was able to reassure them. Elijah had already appeared in the person of John the Baptist. Their last misgivings melted away. They were caught up in the glow and enthusiasm of a dominating personality whose sole power rested in his appeal to the spirit. Henceforth they were prepared to follow their master wherever he ordered them, even into the death-trap of the capital city.

It is hardly necessary for me to say that I find my colleague's account of the Transfiguration quite inadequate from the Christian point of view. To interpret it, as he does, so largely in terms of its impact on the three disciples as if it were something staged entirely for their benefit ignores, for example, the force of St. Luke's references to Moses and Elijah talking with him 'of his decease which he was about to accomplish in Jerusalem'. For the Christian this must remain one of the climactic points in Christ's own understanding of his mission, together with the Temptation and the Agony of Gethsemane. That the incident should have made a profound impact on the three disciples who witnessed it is hardly surprising – though it is interesting to note that here, as in the Garden of Gethsemane, sleep got the better of their intentions. It is also evident that they failed completely to understand what it was all about. Only in retrospect are we able to appreciate the fact that the Transfiguration was in some mysterious way concerned with the consciousness of Jesus himself, that what he now saw clearly to be the inevitable outcome of his ministry was fully in keeping with all that was contained in the Law and the Prophets.   W.W.S.

But first a return must be made to their native Galilee so that they could bid farewell to their families and kinsfolk. Here, too, perhaps, they sold their possessions in accordance with their master's injunction. They re-entered Capernaum for the last time and Jesus, following normal Jewish practice, paid his half-shekel to the Temple fund on the first day of the month Adar, that is, one and a half months before the festival of Passover. At this time a dispute arose among the disciples, who could never quite rise to the selflessness expected of them, as to which should be the greatest in the coming kingdom. Characteristically, and in accordance with the rabbinic saying that, 'little ones receive the presence of the Shechinah [divine presence]', Jesus took hold of a little child and said in effect that he and those who were simple and humble as a child would be the greatest in the kingdom of heaven. Yet he was sufficiently shrewd and realistic not to urge them to make the great renunciation and give up all claims to honour without promising them rich compensation. The man who renounces all worldly possession 'for my name's sake, shall receive a hundred-fold, and shall inherit eternal life', he told them (Matt. xix. 29). But in this kingdom it is not he but his heavenly Father who rewards men according to their due.

Before his departure from Galilee he received a warning from some Pharisees, who knew nothing of his secret claims and still regarded him as one of themselves, to leave the country before he was arrested by Antipas. But Jesus, now merely a bird of passage, no longer feared 'that fox'. He seems to have attempted to make his way to Jerusalem by the direct route through Samaria which, after the expulsion of Archelaus, was governed by the Roman procurator. But the Samaritans were hostile to the Jews and, after a preliminary investigation carried out by two of his bolder disciples, James and John, he decided to cross the Jordan and travel down its eastern bank through the province of Peraea. Here he had no fears, for the country was sparsely inhabited; yet in every village people flocked from a distance and brought their children to catch a glimpse of this 'wonder-Rabbi' whose fame had reached them from the neighbouring Decapolis.

Luke records several incidents as taking place during this journey which are not mentioned by the other Gospel writers. One, when he stayed at the house of a woman named Martha, is of especial interest; for it illustrates Jesus' commendation of the spiritual, contemplative life as something more precious than the 'busyness' of the daily round with all its anxieties and cares. When Martha complained that her sister Mary had sat at Jesus' feet and left her to serve alone, Jesus answered: 'Martha, Martha, thou art anxious and troubled about many things: but one thing is needful: for Mary hath chosen the good part, which shall not be taken away from her' (Luke x. 41–42).

As the party came south and approached Jerusalem there were signs of nervousness among the disciples and Jesus had constantly to encourage them and lead the way. They recrossed the Jordan and entered Jericho, where they were met by a large crowd. According to Luke, Jesus stayed at the house of a wealthy tax-gatherer, Zacchaeus, and as usual offended many of his fellow-Jews by consorting with 'sinners'. Jesus took the precisely opposite view, and when Zacchaeus spontaneously gave up half of his wealth to the poor and made restitution for wrongful exaction, declared that 'he [the tax-gatherer] also is a son of Abraham'.

It was on the way from Jericho to Jerusalem that Jesus, according to Mark, was first addressed as the 'Son of David'.[1] This was the title used by a blind beggar who claimed that his sight had been miraculously restored. It is evidence that Jesus' secret claim to Messiahship had become known outside the immediate circle of his disciples. Moreover, in spite of protests from the surrounding crowd, he allowed the title to go unchallenged. Perhaps he regarded the incident as a portent of the great revelation which he confidently expected would take place at Jerusalem.

It was five days before the festival of Passover when the little band reached the outskirts of the city and stayed at the eastern suburb of Bethphage (House of Figs). Jesus made up his mind to enter Jerusalem in a way that would intimate to the people that the Messiah had indeed arrived. In this, as in many of his actions during the remaining days of his life, he showed his keen sense of the dramatic. Old Testament prophecy and apocalyptic literature generally were full of allusions to the great advent, and in order to obtain the necessary sanctions and impress his Jewish contemporaries he must suit his behaviour to the sacred word. Zechariah had foretold that the Messiah would come 'lowly, and riding upon an ass, even upon a colt the foal of an ass'. Accordingly Jesus, renouncing all pretensions to the role of conquering hero, procured

---

[1] See also Matt. ix. 27, xii. 23, xv. 22.

a colt on which his disciples, like the officers of Jehu of old, placed their garments for a saddle. On this he mounted and started on what proved to be a triumphal entry. People strewed the way before him with their garments and branches of trees. They greeted him with the familiar verse from Psalm cxviii: 'Hosanna (O Save)![1] Blessed be he that cometh in the name of the Lord.' Some naturally looked at him in perplexity and asked who he was. The reply came that he was Jesus, a Galilean prophet. Others cried out that the kingdom of David, their father, had indeed arrived.

It is recorded by Luke that, like Scipio at Carthage, Jesus wept as he looked at the city and thought of the awful fate that – unless this passage was a late addition – he somehow foresaw would befall it. This could not have been his first visit to Jerusalem since he came to manhood, for it is scarcely credible that as an orthodox Jew he had not at some time in his life carried out the religious injunction: 'Three times a year shall all thy males appear before the Lord thy God in the place which he shall choose' (Deut. xvi. 16). But at this period he was in a tense and highly emotional state, and the fate which overhung the Jewish capital was no doubt connected in his mind with his own ordeal. In any case he did not think it safe to stay within its walls and after a brief visit to the Temple he withdrew for the night into the suburb of Bethany. Here he is said to have stayed at the house of a leper. This is inherently improbable as the rules concerning lepers were very strict and they were forbidden to live in residential areas. Perhaps there was confusion in the original Hebrew gospel between the words 'leper' (tsaru-a) and 'humble' (tsanu-a), and he may actually have stayed at the house of 'Simon the lowly', who may have been an Essene.

Luke, describing an earlier episode, wrote that he stayed with Simon the Pharisee, and he tells the beautiful story of the harlot who came in and anointed his feet with myrrh, wept over them, dried them with her hair and kissed them. Something similar seems to have happened at Bethany. When Jesus sat at meat a woman came in with a cruse of spikenard which she poured over

[1] This form of greeting, and still more the mention of palm trees in the Johannine account, suggests that the entry took place at Tabernacles rather than Passover. If so, the subsequent events, instead of being crowded into a few days, may actually have spread over six months.

his head. Those sitting with him were indignant at her waste and extravagance, and said that the scent was worth three hundred dinars, which might have been distributed among the poor. But Jesus praised her generous conduct, adding certain memorable words which clearly reflected his present mood: 'Ye have the poor always with you, and whensoever ye will ye can do them good: but me ye have not always' (Mark xiv. 7).

On his way to Jerusalem the next day (three days before Passover) occurred the curious episode of the fig tree. It was early in the year for fruit, but Jesus was hungry and when he saw this tree from a distance he hoped to find on it some figs sufficiently ripe to eat. In fact he found nothing but leaves, and in his disappointment and exasperation he denounced the tree, saying that it should never bear fruit again. Next day, as they passed the same spot, Peter pointed out to him that for some reason the tree showed signs of withering. Jesus, in an access of remorse and acute self-criticism, with his unique gifts of improving the occasion, warned the disciples of the dangers of spiritual pride, of invoking heavenly power without forgiveness in their hearts. Perhaps this is not a historical incident but a parable (see Luke xiii. 6–9) which has crept into the narrative.

On this day Jesus performed the most daring and dramatic act of his life, and one which more than anything else caused his ultimate downfall. At a time when pilgrims were flocking to Jerusalem from all parts of the country and swelling the crowds who always thronged the Temple courts, he violently removed those who in his opinion were desecrating the sacred precinct. He cleared the Temple of the money-changers and those who trafficked in the sacrificial animals. In so doing he dealt a serious blow at the priesthood, for it was from this source that they drew a large revenue. They now saw themselves confronted not only with a popular Pharisaic preacher whose doctrine was dangerous to established priestly religion, but with a determined and implacable foe of their own authority and vested interests.

For it must be remembered that in performing this act Jesus had the best elements of the population behind him. It is clear from several passages in the Talmud that trafficking in the Temple precincts was quite contrary to Pharisaic practice. Money-changing was, indeed, a necessity, since the pilgrims often came from afar and used many varieties of coinage. But it was forbidden to bring

money within the Temple court and the sale of doves and pigeons
originally took place on the Mount of Olives. In Herod's time,
however, jurisdiction over the Temple had passed into the hands
of the Sadducees and all sorts of abuses had crept in. In his
attempt to stop these by violent methods Jesus must have had a
large crowd of supporters, including the Pharisaic element whose
long pent-up indignation was now given practical expression.
Their passions were no doubt inflamed by Jesus' skilful use of a
famous passage from the Prophet Isaiah: 'Is it not written, My
house shall be called a house of prayer for all the nations? but ye
have made it a den of robbers' (Mark xi. 17).

We can imagine the excitement aroused in Jerusalem by this
bold act of insubordination. It could hardly have passed unnoticed
by the Roman administration, for the chief priests were at this
time their own creatures and almost an agency of political control.
The priests themselves must have felt deep resentment, but they
feared to arrest Jesus while he could command such strong support.
In any case he returned to Bethany for the night, outside their
immediate reach.

So far it seemed that Jesus had gained a measure of popular
success, but from now onwards he steadily lost ground. He
returned next day to the Temple and became involved in various
disputes with the priests and other sections of the people in the
Temple court. When asked by the chief priest and Scribes on
what authority he had acted the previous day, he referred them to
his great predecessor, John the Baptist, implying that his action
had both divine authority and popular support. By use of the
parable method he showed that, as the Messiah, he acted by pre-
scriptive right and they had no power to kill him. If they were
surprised that such an exalted personage should appear in the
guise of a Galilean carpenter, let them remember the text: 'The
stone which the builders rejected is become the head of the corner'
(Ps. cxviii).

In spite of this seemingly arrogant attitude, very like that of
Socrates at his trial, the priests did not yet feel strong enough to
take action and adroitly attempted to lower Jesus' prestige in the
eyes of the people. The main interest of a large section of them in
the Messiah was a practical one. Could he free them from the
hated Roman yoke? It seems that at this time certain Pharisees,
always famous for their dialectical skill, were put up with the

object of placing Jesus in an impossible dilemma. They asked him whether it was lawful, i.e. in accordance with Torah, to pay tribute to Caesar. The implications of this question were deeply significant, for Roman rule was regarded at this period as the antithesis of the kingdom of God. If Jesus replied that it was unlawful, he would be regarded as a rebel and embroil himself with the Roman authorities. If, on the other hand, he condoned the paying of tribute and thus by implication supported Roman rule, his claims to be the Messiah would be proved a mockery and his hold on the people seriously weakened.

His reply, as he took hold of a Roman denarius and pointed to the figure of the Emperor engraved on it, started in the form of a question: 'Whose is this image and superscription?' And when they said, 'Caesar's', he gave them the injunction: 'Render therefore unto Caesar the things that are Caesar's; and unto God the things that are God's' (Matt. xxii. 20–21). In a sense this was a masterly evasion. Jesus attempted to show himself to be a true servant of the King of Kings as well as a law-abiding citizen. But from that moment the magnetism of his influence was perceptibly diminished. The people no doubt expected a much more forthright declaration of hostility to Rome from the lips of their champion, and they began from now onwards to distrust his Messianic pretensions. It was a clever move on the part of the priests, who proved that Jesus, far from being a Zealot who would secure Jewish freedom, was uninterested in the oppression they were suffering from Roman tyranny.

But there were other elements among the people who believed as little in the use of force against Rome as Jesus himself. These, as we have seen, were interested in the spiritual aspects of Messianism, and it might have been expected that Jesus would do everything in his power to court their favour.

Unfortunately, whether by design, because he was convinced that his task required him to play a lonely part and would suffer from any group affiliation, or merely through lack of diplomatic skill, his subsequent conduct only led to their complete alienation. He showed himself an opponent of the Sadducees, who no doubt welcomed his attitude of non-violence to Rome, by asserting his belief in the resurrection of the dead. This, as well as his remark to a Scribe who supported his teaching about the first of all the commandments – 'Thou art not far from the kingdom of God' –

committed him unmistakably to the Pharisaic fold. He gave a further confirmation by his answers to the question as to whether the Messiah must be of Davidic descent. This was the commonly accepted view and accounts for the attempts made by Matthew and Luke to prove that Jesus' father was descended from the house of David. But the Pharisees admitted the principle that the Messiah need not be of Davidic stock (as is shown early in the next century by Rabbi Akibah's support of Bar Kokhbah), and in claiming that the son of a Galilean carpenter could be the Messiah Jesus was again asserting his Pharisaic alignment. Yet he forthwith turned and denounced this sect of which he was a member. They made, he said, a parody of their religion; they 'desire to walk in long robes [tallithim], and to have salutations in the market place, and chief seats in the synagogues and chief places at feasts; they which devour widows' houses, and for a pretence make long prayers'. They are reserved for 'greater condemnation' (Mark xii. 38–40). And thus, having deliberately provoked the popular religious party, he ended the day with a prophecy that the Temple would be destroyed, and, at least according to some of the evidence, gave the impression that he would pull it down with his own hands and build a spiritual Temple in its place. This was no doubt the the language of hyperbole common to apocalyptic utterances, but all the religious parties were sensitive about the Temple, which held a peculiar place in the affections of the people, and by this deliberate use of shock tactics Jesus probably alienated the last remnants of his supporters.

The rest of his final discourse delivered on the Mount of Olives, with its magnificent imagery and flights of poetic fancy, conformed to the usual pattern of apocalyptic prophecy. The old order was to pass away and the kingdom of heaven was 'nigh even at the doors'. Such phrases as 'the pangs of the Messiah' were a commonplace in the Talmudic Baraitas and one, even describing 'the week when the son of David comes', speaks of famines and wars and 'rumours'. This was the very language used by Jesus and showed how completely he had by this time identified himself with that small group that combined Pharisaism with apocalyptic dreams (see p. 50). It was the renewal of his conviction that the role he was called upon to play was to be lifted from the worldly to the transcendental. He had 'immortal longings' in him.

Jesus had done enough to provoke the implacable hostility of all the Jewish authorities, and on this day (probably the fourth of the week and two days before Passover) the Sadducaic leaders deter-mined to arrest him 'with subtlety' and have him put to death. It would seem from the Johannine account (xviii. 3–12) that at this point they did actually approach Pontius Pilate and secure a promise of Jesus' condemnation; and that he furnished them with a military tribune and a detachment of soldiers in order to effect the arrest. The Synoptic picture, however, is rather different, and suggests that they were still frightened of the people and the large crowds which had assembled in Jerusalem, and decided to post-pone taking action until after the festival. But an unexpected development played into their hands and hastened Jesus' arrest.

Among his disciples, as we have seen, was one non-Galilean, Judas, of the town of Kerioth in Judea. He was probably therefore a better educated and more critical follower of his master than the rest. The motives which led him to betray Jesus at this moment are necessarily conjectural, but there is nothing to show hitherto that he was a man of special perfidy or baseness of character, or that he was any less ardent than the others in his support of Jesus' cause. It is therefore unlikely that his aims were purely mercenary, as the Gospel story suggests. More probably he had become dis-illusioned about his leader's claims, and began to think that he was one of those false Messiahs or prophets or 'dreamers of dreams' who, according to the Deuteronomic code (Deut. xiii. 5), must be put to death. After all, there were on the face of it many contradic-tions in Jesus' teaching about observance of the Law, about the use of violence, about the right attitude towards authority, which must have puzzled even his greatest admirers. Especially, the appar-ent failure of his mission would have shaken their confidence, for he had in no way changed the political scene or brought any allevia-tion of their suffering to his downtrodden people. Judas may have been one of those who applied this test to Messianic claims. Added to all this, there was the fear of sudden arrest by the authorities shared not only by all the disciples but by Jesus him-self, who returned each night to Bethany and, except when surrounded by a throng of supporters, kept his movements as secret as possible.

It was this man who reported Jesus' hiding-place to the High Priest and the local Jewish authorities and accelerated their action in arresting him. At what moment he did this is uncertain, but it was probably not until after the Seder, or Eve of Passover, ritual supper. There is great confusion with regard to the chronology of these fateful days, and this meal appears to have taken place on the Thursday evening, though the festival itself did not commence until sunset on the Friday.

It is an interesting and important fact with regard to this vexed question of chronology that, at least in regard to the events of this last night, there is good ground for supposing that the Fourth Gospel is more reliable than the Synoptists. According to St. John the day which began at sunset on Thursday was the 'day of the preparation for the Passover'. If this was in fact the case, then 'the last supper' would have been the normal evening meal, which on the eve of the festival might well have been preceded by the familiar Kiddush or sanctification of bread and wine. This would have meant also a coincidence between the time of the crucifixion and the killing of the Passover lambs in the Temple, and there would have been no desecration of the Sabbath by the crucifying of three persons, even at the hands of the Romans. But we cannot be sure. W.W.S.

The ceremonial had to be carried out within Jerusalem and Jesus made private arrangements with a simple water-carrier to allow him and his disciples to celebrate in an upper chamber. The *mazzoth* (unleavened cakes) would be broken and passed round for consumption, and four cups of wine drunk with suitable liturgical blessings. The story of the first sacrifice of the Paschal lamb and the liberation from Egypt would be rehearsed. The eating of the bread of affliction and the *maror* (bitter herbs) as well as the sacrifice of the lamb may well have reminded Jesus of his own predicament. With his belief in the imminence of a new order he may well have thought this his last Seder. He therefore spoke to his disciples of the meal in sacramental terms and urged them to cherish its memory after he was gone. But the ceremony ended joyously according to custom with the singing of the Hallel psalms.

According to the Deuteronomic law the night had to be spent in Jerusalem, but it was permitted to change places within the city precincts. 'They may eat in one place and spend the night in another', says the Talmud. At this time, though Jesus had no certain premonitions that death was imminent, his actions show that he was in great fear of arrest. He decided to move to Gethsemane on the Mount of Olives, which was within the city's limits but farthest from its centre. He seems to have arranged for some armed protection in case his hiding-place was discovered. There is a hint that he promised his disciples that he would soon return to Galilee.

To the Christian this paragraph must seem strange indeed. The idea that Jesus retired to Gethsemane for security reasons bears little relation to the impression conveyed by the Gospels themselves, where he is represented as being much more alive to the inevitabilities of the situation than A.I.P. suggests. Indeed, it was to prepare himself more completely for what he had long since recognized as the logical consequence of the way he had chosen from the outset of his ministry that he retired to the quiet of a garden at this critical moment. W.W.S.

The whole human drama of this intensely tragic figure now came swiftly to a head. Followed by only three of his disciples, Peter, James and John, Jesus retired to a lonely spot to pray. He was suffering from utter dejection and nervous prostration, the direct result of the strain of the last few days and the consciousness of the imminent danger in which he stood. He told them that his soul was 'exceeding sorrowful, even unto death', and bade them: 'Abide ye here, and watch.' He went a little way apart and, falling on his face, prayed that this evil hour might pass away from him and that his Father might remove from him the cup of affliction. He returned to find his disciples asleep and after a mild reproof, addressed especially to Peter, he urged them again to watch and pray lest, through neglect, they fall into temptation and imperil their whole cause; 'for the spirit indeed is willing, but the flesh is weak'. But they had drunk and eaten freely at the Seder table, and he returned twice more to find them asleep. He came to the bitter conclusion that he could rely on them no more (Matt. xxvi. 38–44).

Once again I find myself impelled to go on record against what seems to me a serious over-simplification. 'Dejection and nervous prostration' will, I am confident, strike many, if not most, of our Christian readers as a very inadequate diagnosis, while to attribute the sleepiness of the three disciples to their having 'drunk and eaten freely at the Seder table' is to ignore both the sense of strain and anxiety under which

they were suffering and also the surely not irrelevant fact that, as I
mentioned in an earlier note, the same three disciples slept at the time
of the Transfiguration.   W.W.S.

Meanwhile Judas had gone off secretly to inform Caiaphas, the
High Priest, and the Jewish authorities of Jesus' hiding-place.
Caiaphas was of the family of Annas, much hated by the people,
according to the Talmud, because of their violence and secret
denunciations. 'Woe is me for the House of Annas, woe is me for
their secret whisperings. . . . For they are the High Priests and
their sons the Treasurers: their sons-in-law are the Temple officers
and their servants beat the people with staves.' So runs a popular
ballad. Caiaphas himself had been appointed by the Procurator,
Valerius Gratus, in A.D. 18 and he remained in office for nearly
eighteen years, a tribute rather to diplomatic astuteness than
spiritual sincerity.

This man saw his opportunity of getting rid of one whom he
regarded as a popular agitator, likely not only to threaten the
established hierarchy on account of his religious teaching, but,
more serious still, to embroil them with the Roman authorities.
He immediately summoned his court, a political Sanhedrin (see
p. 63) composed of the Sadducees and their scribes (for the
Pharisees now disappear from the scene), whose main function was
to keep a jealous watch on behalf of their Roman masters. This
court decided to arrest Jesus, and they sent off a 'police' force for
this purpose which accompanied Judas to Gethsemane.

The exact details of what followed can never be known for
certain. By a pre-arranged signal, possibly a kiss, which was the
usual form of greeting, Judas conveyed Jesus' identity to his
escort. There was some show of resistance on the part of the disciples and, according to the Gospel account, one of them cut off
the ear of one of the High Priest's servants. Jesus may have
rebuked them, and the superb aphorism quoted by Matthew –
'All they that take the sword shall perish with the sword' – is in
keeping with much of his teaching. What is undoubtedly historical
is that the resistance failed, that the disciples fled to avoid capture
and that Jesus, with a heart-breaking appeal on his lips – 'Are ye
come out as against a robber with swords and staves to seize me?
I sat daily in the temple teaching, and ye took me not' – allowed
himself to be led away to the High Priest's house alone. Such was

the general panic that one of his followers, a mere boy, rushed off naked leaving the sheet in which he had slept in the hands of the guards (Matt. xxvi. 47-56).

The only disciple who followed Jesus, and that 'afar off', was Peter, and it is probably through him that we have an account of the confused events of the next few hours. We read in Matthew that Peter came into the court of the High Priest's house and sat with the guards warming himself by the fire. One of the female servants (or the gate-keeper) recognized him as a follower of Jesus and his Galilean accent nearly gave him away. He escaped arrest by asserting that he did not know Jesus.

Either that night or early next morning there was some sort of trial or investigation. It was certainly not conducted according to Jewish or Pharisaic law but resembled much more the kind of political frame-up which has become so common in modern totalitarian states. The Boethusian and Sadducean priests were mere puppets of the Government and no doubt genuinely afraid that a continuation of Jesus' activities might lead to wholesale reprisals on the part of the ruthless Procurator. There was, therefore, little pretence of judicial enquiry, and the prisoner was in fact regarded as guilty before the proceedings started.

The chief indictments which the Sanhedrin brought against Jesus were (i) that he was planning to destroy the Temple; (ii) that he was perverting the nation and preventing them from paying tribute to Caesar by asserting that he was the Messiah (and therefore King). Throughout this enquiry Jesus remained silent, and though witnesses were called they 'agreed not together'. The High Priest thereupon put the direct question to him: 'Art thou the Christ?' To this Jesus, who was by now more convinced than ever of his Messiahship, answered in the affirmative, amplifying his statement with apocalyptic claims: 'And ye shall see the Son of man sitting at the right hand of power, and coming with the clouds of heaven' (Mark xiv. 61–62).

To the High Priest and the Sadducean court this must have sounded something like blasphemy. How could a Galilean carpenter dare to style himself 'Son of man' – could any good thing come out of Nazareth? – and pretend that he was the Lord's anointed servant and therefore 'King of the Jews'? Caiaphas rent his garments, as was the custom when the judge heard blasphemous words, and though there may have been some supporters of Jesus present (such as Joseph of Arimathea) he received a death sentence from the court.

At this time, as we have seen, Jewish courts had no power to carry out the death penalty on a political issue, so that the case had to be referred to the Roman Governor. During the Passover festival Pilate took up his residence at the Palace of Herod (the Praetorium), which contained a large barracks for his garrison. Here, on information received from the High Priest, he summoned Jesus to trial on the charge of insurrection. (The religious charge of blasphemy would scarcely have interested the Roman authorities and was quickly dropped.) At this point it is well to remember that the Evangelists, writing many years later during or after the Jewish revolt of A.D. 66–70, were concerned to exonerate the Roman administration and fasten the blame for what occurred on the enemies of Rome, the Jews. It is inherently improbable that Pilate wavered in his judgment or sought to evade responsibility. Everything we know of this ruthless man seems to show that he would unhesitatingly condemn anyone suspected of rebellion against the state. He was never particularly squeamish where Jewish lives were concerned, and we may be sure that his quislings would be careful to furnish him with the most incriminating evidence before they handed Jesus over.

The stories of his referring the case to Antipas on the grounds that Jesus was a Galilean, of his wife's dream, of his releasing Barabbas, a Zealot, at the people's request, when he wished to release Jesus,[1] may be regarded as apocryphal. Especially suspect is Matthew's assertion that Pilate washed his hands, 'saying, I am innocent of the blood of this righteous man: see ye to it. And all the people answered and said, His blood be on us and on our children' (Matt. xxvii. 25).

The trial was, presumably, conducted according to normal Roman procedure. The 'people' were not present, though a small crowd may have gathered outside the Praetorium. Pilate accused Jesus of setting himself up as 'King of the Jews'. Jesus' evasive answer, 'Thou sayest', and the rest of the evidence convinced Pilate that he, like so many others, was a potential danger to Roman authority. No doubt Pilate thought of him as just another

[1] No such custom of liberating prisoners before Passover is known to Josephus or any Jewish writer. The story probably had its origins in Eastern folk-lore.

Galilean Zealot and was incapable of making nice distinctions between the different Jewish religious beliefs. He ordered him to be summarily executed by the Roman method of crucifixion and handed him over to the guards.

There is not much more to relate of this painful and tragic event, which, as we can tell from Cicero's speech against Verres, had its counterpart in so many of the Roman provinces, when a repressive and cruel governor was responsible for the administration. Execution was preceded by scourging, which inflamed the naked body and caused it to bleed. There was the mocking of the victim by the coarse legionaries, and in Jesus' case, as he had claimed to be 'King of the Jews', they dressed him in purple and put a sham crown on his head. There were other and worse indignities to which he had to submit. Finally, dressing him once more in his own clothes, and making him carry his own cross, they led him from the Praetorium to a skull-shaped hill called Golgotha.

He was followed by a crowd of people, some of whom were would-be sympathizers. Among these were a number of women, including certain Galileans who had followed him from his home and remained with him till the end. It was by one of them, presumably, that he was offered a cup of wine mingled with frankincense to deaden the pain he would have to endure. Most of the other details described in the Gospel account – that the soldiers drew lots for his clothes, that he was crucified between two thieves, that one of the soldiers stretched up a reed bearing a sponge filled with vinegar – so closely resemble specific prophecies in the Old Testament that they must be regarded with suspicion. But the words he uttered in the agony of the death struggle, 'My God, my God, why hast thou forsaken me?', have a pathetically genuine ring and show the bitterness of despair into which this poor, helpless, innocent man had been driven. Perhaps (who can tell?) he had pinned his hopes on some final supernatural deliverance.

At this point my colleague and I have found ourselves faced with a crux. And while this is not the place to enter in any detail into its nature or the reasons for it, I feel bound to say that the picture of a 'poor, helpless, innocent man' driven to 'the bitterness of despair' does not really meet the situation either from a historical or from a Christian point of view. (See also my note on p. 100.)   W.W.S.

Nevertheless there is evidence that, even in the last agonizing moments, his deep, indomitable faith sustained him. The main theme of the 22nd Psalm from which he had quoted was confidence in God as the great deliverer of all innocent sufferers. And Luke records that at the end, with characteristic magnanimity, he prayed for his persecutors: 'Father, forgive them; for they know not what they do'; and that he died with an utterance of supreme resignation on his lips: 'Father, into thy hands I commend my spirit.'

After his death the *titulus* (charge) was written according to custom on the cross-beam: 'This is Jesus, the King of the Jews.' One of the elders of the Sanhedrin, probably at the request of the disciples, asked Pilate for the body of Jesus. After death had been confirmed by a centurion, he was allowed to take it and, having wrapped it in burial clothes, consigned it to a private tomb where the last rites were no doubt administered.

Such was the mortal end of yet one more Jewish martyr whose only crime was that, in his whole-hearted zeal for the kingdom of God, he failed to pay lip service to the kingdom of man.

CHAPTER IX

TEACHINGS: I. TRANSCENDENTAL

W E have seen in the last chapter how a blameless man was put to death, like so many in that and perhaps every age, as the victim of an inexorable authoritarian machine. This had been created through the kind of unholy alliance between priestcraft and ruler, based on an identity of interest, which centuries previously had been broken by the Deuteronomic reformation (see p. 14) but was again operating with full force after the Roman occupation. It was the precursor of that ruthless and vicious state-church association which through so much of European history has tended to crush the independence and stifle the conscience of the individual man. As a rule the victims, for all their suffering, left little behind by which their fellow men could remember them.

In a sense the crucifixion was the end of Jesus too. He was soon forgotten by all except a handful of followers, and his condemnation and death were hardly noted by contemporary historians. Compare the sensation aroused by the condemnation of Socrates four centuries earlier, or the murder of Julius Caesar in the previous century, and you will get some measure of the obscurity in which the whole life and career of Jesus were shrouded. His fate, indeed, was not dissimilar to that which befell countless of his compatriots during the last unhappy years of their political existence.

Yet it is true to say, in a sense which can be applied to few other events, that it was but a beginning. The life and death of Jesus have literally changed history. The distinction between B.C. and A.D. is not a purely artificial one, for nothing was quite the same in the era that followed. And this can only be explained in terms of what Jesus himself did and taught.

Yet in trying to assess his teachings, or 'witness' as it is rightly called, a biographer finds himself in immediate difficulties. It is impossible to give a systematic account of his teaching or codify it in any coherent form; and this for several reasons. First, he never set out to give his generation a new philosophy or meta-physical concept. He was not an original thinker or innovator, if this is the right description of men like Plato or Schopenhauer or Karl Marx. His genius lay, rather, in the intensity of his experience and his capacity to communicate it to his fellow men.

Again, there is a certain inconsistency in his teaching, character-istic of men whose perception and sense of vocation are emotionally informed. Most of us, who live at cooler temperatures, find it difficult to understand a man whose whole life was dominated by a passion for righteousness and a tender yearning to give and receive love. We learn to take the rebuffs of our fellow men with a certain complacency, a shrug of the shoulders; but the artist in living or, rather, in loving, is a man of higher sensitivity, and his encounter with the grim crudities of life is apt to plunge him into moods of frustration and despair. Jesus was just such an artist, and the dark patches are not absent from his canvas. When we come across them in terms of violent intolerance or bitter denun-ciation, we must remember that we are not dealing with a dis-passionate or scientific observer of men, but with an impulsive, intuitive mind, not always sure of direction in the practical affairs of life, but convinced of the rightness of its own conviction and perplexed in the extreme at the motives of those who failed to share it. Such a man both thought and spoke in hyperbole.

On this chapter I hardly know where to begin, let alone what to say. For while I am tempted to rush into indignant comment here and there – it is not easy, for example, for a Christian to take kindly to the attribution to Jesus of 'violent intolerance or bitter denunciation' – I am held in check by two considerations, to one of which I have already referred several times in these notes. This is the fact that, if I seem here to be confronted with a Jesus strangely different from the one I have learned to know and love, it is because A.I.P.'s approach to him is influenced consciously and, perhaps to a far greater extent than he himself realizes, unconsciously by certain presuppositions which to me would be quite unacceptable.

But the second consideration that holds me in check is the feeling that if I start to comment on this detail I shall perforce have to comment on that also, with the result that my notes would be as long as, if not longer than, the chapter itself. But apart altogether from considerations of space this would not help very much, for the more I think about it, the more I am driven back on the conclusion that the differences between us here have to do, not with the interpretation of this or that detail, but with the fundamental nature of our respective approaches.

I come back therefore to the now familiar point that respect for the genuineness and the sincerity of A.I.P.'s approach places upon me the obligation of trying as best I can to understand and appreciate how and why he has come to feel as he does. I am strengthened in this resolve by the fact that I believe he feels very much the same about my approach. This at least is certain, that neither of us has yet seen the whole truth. In the meantime it is reasonable to hope that each of us may still learn something from the other.　　　　W.W.S.

There are two more reasons why Jesus' teaching does not easily submit to a systematic analysis. Throughout his ministry he assumed in his hearers the knowledge and practice of the Judaism in which he and they had been reared. In most of what he said he was merely echoing or emphasizing the best teachings of Moses and the Prophets, of Psalmist or contemporary Rabbi. He came, to use his own words, not to abolish the Law but to complete it. We cannot, as has already been stated, begin to understand his message – and this is especially true of that part of it which might be called 'new' – unless we have studied the religious background which both the teacher and his disciples took for granted.

A final difficulty is in regard to the authenticity of many utterances which have been put into his mouth. As has been shown in a previous chapter, we are dependent for our knowledge of Jesus' life and teaching on men who had had no personal contact with him and who wrote their accounts a generation after his death. By that time a new religion had grown up of which he was the centre and, as so often happens with great men, there was a certain accumulation of legendary matter which tended to obscure and distort the original personality. Moreover, in their zeal for the new faith the writers were often anxious to discredit the old, and in some cases, no doubt under the stress of persecution, engaged in a violent polemic against the very people to which Jesus belonged. A good instance of this is found in the account of the Crucifixion given by Luke. A modern Christian scholar, commenting on xxiii. 20–21 in *The Cambridge Bible*, writes: 'We see merely the Evangelists' determination to make all the Jews appear in the most odious light possible.' And again: 'Another quite unlikely trait in a narrative which it is impossible to accept as history.' Thus, from a historical point of view, parts of the Gospel account must be regarded as suspect and any attempt to formulate the teaching of Jesus entails a certain eclecticism, based on literary and historical research as well as inherent probability.

In spite of what I have just said about not commenting on details in this chapter, I cannot refrain from observing that the opening of this paragraph affords a good example of what seems to me to be one of the limitations of A.I.P.'s approach to this whole subject. For while I fully agree that we must make allowance for the accretion of 'a certain amount of legendary material' and the frequent tendency of converts from one faith to another to do less than justice to that from which they have turned, I think he himself dismisses too easily the importance of the traditions, both oral and written, which go back to some at least of those who were not only contemporaries of Jesus but themselves knew him intimately. Thus, as he himself has pointed out in an earlier chapter, there is very good ground for believing that Mark was not simply a man who had no personal knowledge of Jesus and wrote a generation after his death, but was in fact a close friend and disciple of Peter from whom he received what he wrote in his Gospel.

But for the Christian there is a still further consideration to be taken into account, namely the claim that it was the Lord himself who 'caused the Holy Scriptures to be written for our learning'. This is not to suggest that there is anything magical about them, or that they are free from the limitations of error imposed by the imperfections of those through whom the 'good news' was passed on. It is, however, to affirm that in relation to these, as indeed to the writings of the Old Testament, there is always the factor of the divine initiative to be taken into account. And the evidence for that, many would claim with equal sincerity to find precisely where A.I.P. himself seems not to see it, namely in the very character of the records themselves. The surprising thing, after all, is less that they bear traces of the human limitations of their writers, than that they should present a record and a portrait which has proved so convincing to so many for so long.   W.W.S.

In spite of all this the main ideas which inspired his msssage are abundantly clear, and admit of little or no controversy. Pervading all his teaching was a sense of the fatherhood of God. In this Jesus

was a typical Jew. He never compromised with the principle of
God's unity, his limitless power, his all-pervading love. Never for
a moment did it occur to him to equate himself or any other
human being with the transcendent nature of the Deity. When he
was hailed as 'Good Master', he exclaimed: 'Why callest thou me
good? none is good, save one, even God.' He was acutely conscious,
too, of his own powerlessness and helplessness except through
the saving grace of his heavenly Father. In moments of acute
distress he turned to him as the only redeemer. 'Abba, Father, all
things are possible unto thee; remove this cup from me; howbeit
[this, with sublime courage and resignation] not what I will, but
what thou wilt.' And his cry of despair on the cross, 'My God,
my God, why hast thou forsaken me?' shows his utter dependence
on the 'divinity which shapes our ends'. In all this he was the
expounder of traditional Jewish doctrine.

There were, however, two aspects of his teaching or, rather, of
his thinking about God, which departed to some extent from the
main pattern of Jewish theology; or perhaps it would be truer to
say that by a new emphasis they threw certain strands in that
pattern into bold relief. We have seen that there were sections of
the Jewish people who, under the influence of apocalyptic prophecies, expected that the old order would soon disappear and be
succeeded by a reign of peace and brotherhood known as the
kingdom of God. They differed as to how the new era was to be
brought about, but all agreed that its inauguration would be the
work of a messenger of God, a Messiah, whether by this term they
meant a divine or a human personality.

Now Jesus, at least after his meeting with John, regarded this
cosmic metamorphosis as imminent in the highest degree. 'This
generation shall not pass away, till all these things be accomplished,'
he asserted. And again: 'There be some here of them that stand
by which shall in no wise taste of death, till they see the kingdom
of God come with power.' Thus not only did he believe, like other
Pharisaic apocalyptics, that the great transformation would come
through some divine or supernatural process, but there was also
in his mind the strong conviction that the process was already
starting. This view, as we shall see, profoundly affected the tone
and quality of much of his ethical teaching and gave it its markedly
paradoxical character.

The second fresh and partly un-Hebraic element in his thinking had to do with his personal relationship with God. We have seen that at some point in his career, perhaps after his meeting with John, he came to the conclusion that he himself was God's appointed messenger, the Messiah, through whose agency the old order would change, giving place to new. It is never possible to know for certain the mental processes working in the mind of another man, particularly when he is a man of baffling genius, but it seems reasonably clear that before this conviction came upon him, perhaps even in childhood, Jesus had an exceptionally strong sense of personal kinship with his heavenly Father. He made, for instance, far more use than did the Rabbis and Pharisees of such expressions as 'Father', 'my Father in heaven'. The same sort of feeling was common enough among the Psalmists and Prophets, but the general trend of Jewish teaching was to claim this special relationship with the divine for the whole people of Israel. Jesus seems at times, if we can judge from much of his language, to have appropriated this divine election to himself. Though he never fully identified himself with God, yet he claimed to possess an exceptional awareness of God's nature and purpose which could only arise from the conviction that he stood nearer to him than any other person.

Of these two new elements or new emphases in religious teaching it was the first, the belief in the imminence of the Kingdom, that led to the extreme note of urgency in much of Jesus' teaching. He was afraid that it would come before people were aware of it or prepared for it. It would come suddenly like the great flood in the time of Noah, or 'like a thief in the night':

> I say unto you, In that night, there shall be two men in one bed; the one shall be taken, and the other shall be left. There shall be two women grinding together; the one shall be taken, and the other shall be left (Luke xvii. 34–35).
> Therefore be ye also ready: for in an hour that ye think not the Son of man cometh (Matt. xxiv. 44).

The eschatological teaching of Jesus had, therefore, more than one aspect. Sometimes he seems to have regarded the coming of 'the kingdom' as a divine intervention in human affairs heralded by the appearance of the 'Son of man' in clouds of glory from heaven – and, as we have seen, he came to regard himself as appointed for this particular role. But in another and, for us, a more valuable sense he thought of the kingdom of God as 'within you', as dependent on man's regenerative powers, on his capacity for banishing evil, the cruel and selfish desires which lurk in his heart and cause such widespread oppression and misery. We have here almost an early anticipation of the Marxian paradox. For though Jesus and the apocalyptic school to which he belonged undoubtedly held the determinist view that the coming of God's kingdom was inevitable, yet at the same time he thought that it would be retarded, even unrecognized, in its earthly setting, unless men were prepared for it in their hearts, unless it fell, so to speak, on propitious soil. It is like a grain of mustard seed which grows into a great plant from being the least of all the seeds; or like the leaven concealed in three measures of meal which subsequently leavens the whole; or like the good seed which men plant in the field, and which may be turned to rottenness while the world is asleep. Hence the note of extreme urgency, the desperate cry to repentance, which was characteristic of both John the Baptist and Jesus himself. They threw themselves into the fight for redemption with all the anxious solicitude and untiring energy of doctors fighting to save a human life. To Jesus especially with his tender and enthusiastic, yet diffident, nature the battle was always for something which might be irretrievably lost or won.

That is why there is a strongly ascetic side to his teaching. He insisted that men must give up everything they held dear, 'sell all' and follow him; that is, pursue the life of austerity and resignation. Property, marriage, family relationships – all these might imperil a man's soul and make him unfit for the kingdom of God. The consequence of a rejection of the divine grace assumed in his eyes the most terrifying proportions. The pursuit of selfishness and godless aims would bring the world crashing down in a torrent of destruction. The day of judgment, which would come 'like a thief in the night', would usher in a period of terror and gloom, a world cataclysm in which the old order would be swept away if man continued to disobey God and turned a deaf ear to his warnings. There is no doubt that Jesus saw the doom reserved for man, if he continued to sin, in stark, physical terms.

Of the nature of the kingdom itself he gave little indication, but it may be assumed that he accepted much of the current Jewish, apocalyptic picture. In an age of misery, oppression and sin the people thought of the Messianic kingdom as the reign of goodness and love. No longer would the poor be oppressed, the rich live in luxury and vice. Ungodly tyrants would be overthrown and Israel under the King-Messiah, the suffering servant of the Lord, would be restored to her own. Then, at the sound of the trumpet, there would be a gathering of the exiles from the four corners of the earth, and all nations would flock to the holy mount and become one society 'to do the will of God with a perfect heart'. The Messiah himself, in that day, would stand 'at the right hand of God' and judge both Jews and Gentiles, assigning the righteous to the kingdom and sinners to the fire of hell. This would be followed by the resurrection of the dead; in the first instance of the righteous only but, after a period of purification, of the wicked also, until finally there would be established 'the world to come' wherein 'is neither eating nor drinking, nor fruitfulness, nor begetting of children, nor trafficking, nor jealousy, nor strife', but all should live 'as the angels of the Lord'.

Such were the alternatives which Jesus' followers had in mind when he spoke to them of the coming of the kingdom and the urgent necessity for repentance; and though his insistence on the purely spiritual elements of the promise constituted something comparatively new in the world's teaching, yet he knew the character of his audience and was not above appealing to those poor simple folk in material terms. That is why he promised those who gave up their property 'houses and fields an hundredfold', and told his disciples that they would 'sit on thrones and judge the house of Israel'. But, like no other man before him, he believed with the whole intensity of his being that salvation lay in the individual's willingness to serve his Maker with a perfect heart, and that his every action had an eternal significance in effecting the ultimate regeneration of mankind.

Of the second new element in his teaching, which concerned his personal relation to the divine, much has already been made clear in the short survey of his life and ministry. It is an aspect that is shown as much by his actions and example as in his actual words. Very early in his life he must have felt a special nearness to his Maker and regarded himself as marked out from his fellows for some divinely appointed task. We may even think it doubtful if he could have achieved what he did achieve, or endured what he was called upon to endure, without the reassurance of God's constant presence, without this certainty of divine access and communication. It is almost always the case with the spiritually exalted that they have felt themselves to be in touch with a power that transcends the physical world. Moses realized the presence of God in a burning bush, and it was the turning-point of his career. Socrates tells us that at every crisis of his life he heard the voice of his 'familiar spirit' and practised the art of midwifery in order to bring the word to life. Those who have read Shaw's play on Joan of Arc are familiar with her claim to have gained confidence throughout her life from listening to the voices of the saints. Jesus with his acute sensitivity drew unlimited resources of courage and inspiration from this certainty that God was near him, intimate with him, and loved him as his own child.

It was natural, therefore, that as he came to learn the current notions about God's beloved servant, the Messiah, who had been chosen to suffer for the sins of mankind in order that the world might gain salvation, he began to identify himself with this conception. That is why in a great deal of his teaching about God his own relation to him tended to occupy a central position. He felt that if he could persuade men to identify themselves exclusively with the nature of their heavenly Father, as he himself did, the whole world would be redeemed. It was as though his own particular relation with the divine was an allegory written for the benefit of all men. Hence much the most important aspect of his teaching lay in this stress on what may be called the individualist ethic. The Old Testament Prophets and Psalmists and the contemporary Jewish Rabbis were also intensely concerned with man's behaviour and the necessity of walking uprightly with God. But it was the fate of the whole house of Israel that dominated their thoughts, and their emphasis was, with certain notable exceptions, on a communal ethic and way of life. As we shall see in the next chapter, though geographically his thought never travelled far outside his own national group, owing to his intense concern with the individual soul, Jesus did in fact bring a new universalism into the realm of ideas; or at least he struck with fresh precision a chord only fitfully and tentatively sounded by the early Hebrew Prophets. It came in time to vibrate as the full rich music of total humanity; and this new harmony undoubtedly derived from his conviction that God's kingdom was not some 'far-off, divine event' but an imminent transformation of the world order depending for its realization on a change in the individual man's heart.

CHAPTER X

TEACHINGS: II. ETHICAL

FIRST impressions might suggest that Jesus' belief and teaching about the imminent collapse of the old order and the advent of God's kingdom through supernatural agency would have seriously impaired the value of his message for future generations. Was he just another in that long procession of cranks who have prophesied that the world was coming to an end? In that case, however compelling his call to repentance, its effect would have been merely ephemeral. Some might have mended their ways in the hope of salvation or through fear of 'the everlasting bonfire'; there was always a danger that others might say: 'Let us eat and drink and be merry, for tomorrow we die.' In any case when, in fact, no cosmic revolution came about and the world went on as usual, thus falsifying Jesus' apocalyptic prophecies, it might be thought that the whole of his message would quickly have been forgotten.

That this did not happen but that, on the contrary, he became one of the great teachers of mankind for all time, is due to that other part of his message which tacitly assumed that the present order would continue and that men would go on living pretty much as they did. We must be grateful for this apparent inconsistency in Jesus' outlook, that he was able to live at the same time, so to speak, in two dimensions. For it enabled him to speak to man in practical terms, and to bequeath to posterity an ideal ethic which has stood as a perpetual test of human conduct. His doctrine that 'the kingdom of God is within you', the essentially Hebraic element in his teaching, means more to us today than all those brilliant anticipations of divine intervention in the world order. We are interested in the 'immanence' of the divine spirit rather than its 'imminence'.

One of his great assets in speaking to man about conduct, in pleading with him to reform his ways and follow the will of his Maker, was his gift for very simple, direct and vivid language. Something has been said about his use of parable and forms of speech which even the ignorant could understand. Again and again this method enabled him to invest the world and the dark perplexities of life with rich and hitherto unsuspected meaning. By appealing to man's common experience and the ordinary things of nature, he made his message plain for even the most limited intelligence. He did not, for instance, expatiate on the virtues of magnanimity or the evils of complacency and self-righteousness. Instead, with a few deft touches, he painted the picture of the farmer who possessed a hundred sheep and lost one of them. 'Doth he not leave the ninety and nine in the wilderness, and go after that which is lost, until he find it? And when he hath found it, he layeth it on his shoulders, rejoicing. And when he cometh home, he calleth together his friends and his neighbours, saying unto them, Rejoice with me, for I have found my sheep which was lost' (Luke xv. 4–6). In this way, using language that was 'familiar in their mouths as household words', he adjured men to be forgiving to one another, not to ostracize from society one who had erred and was, therefore, presumed to deserve their reprobation.

With all that A.I.P. has to say in this chapter about the simple, direct and vivid language in which Jesus taught, about his use of parable and metaphor and the brilliance of his word pictures, I am in the fullest possible agreement. I am less happy about his assessment of the content of the teaching thus vividly presented, and of its relation to the person of the teacher himself. In some ways it would be easier to explain the grounds of my uneasiness in a supplementary chapter. I have decided, however, to conform to the pattern we have followed hitherto and to attempt to deal with what I feel to be an overall problem in a series of separate but, I fear, inevitably interrelated footnotes.   W.W.S.

Whenever Jesus wanted to inculcate a particular virtue he used this kind of imagery and showed himself, like many a Rabbi of the Talmudic period, to be a master of metaphor. Man, in his humility and suffering, was called 'the salt of the earth'. His good works are like a candle, not hidden under a bushel, but illuminating the whole house. Hard work and service are commended under the images of tending a fruit tree or finding treasure, importunity in prayer as hammering at the door for loaves of bread. No simile has ever surpassed in its haunting beauty the one in which he appealed for the quiet, untroubled mind: 'Consider the lilies, how they grow: they toil not, neither do they spin; yet I say unto you, even Solomon in all his glory was not arrayed like one of these' (Luke xii. 27). Such brilliant word pictures enabled him to draw on man's imagination and emotional experience and so illuminate the dark places in his mind. They served something of the purpose of Plato's myths, for both men in their different ways had a keen sense of the poetry of life.

It was this imaginative, penetrating quality of Jesus' mind that enabled him as few other men to see life steadily and see it whole, and to give to mankind an absolute ethic based on a perpetual appeal to first principles. He tore, as it were, from men's eyes the veil of artificiality and pretence that obscured the bright vision, bared their hearts and unearthed all the unconscious motives of greed and selfishness and pride which were the mainspring of so much of their action. He showed them what they could be if they lived as their Maker wished them to live and discarded the trivial, momentary triumphs for a life of heavenly grace.

This paragraph, as it seems to me, brings us face to face with a quite fundamental question with which all who are interested in the teaching of Jesus are bound sooner or later to find themselves confronted. It concerns not so much the content of the teaching itself as the person of the teacher. Who was it who could presume to challenge men with what A.I.P. rightly, I think, describes as 'an absolute ethic based on a perpetual appeal to first principles'? What was his authority? (That incidentally was one of the first questions asked by his contemporaries.) And did he really know what he was doing?

This last question is perhaps more far-reaching in its implications than appears at first sight, for it raises the further question whether, not to put too fine a point on it, he was a very foolish or a very wise man. For there are few who can really stand the shock of 'having their hearts bared' and 'all the unconscious motives of greed and selfishness unearthed'. Moreover, to be shown what men 'could be if they lived as their Maker wished them to live' can be a terribly shattering and frustrating experience if we are thinking simply in terms of 'absolute ethics'. It is rather like setting a novice down in Darjeeling, showing him the summit of Everest and telling him to go and climb it. There is a vivid description of what this means in terms of a spiritual initiate in the seventh chapter of St. Paul's letter to the Romans. Sooner or later the end is a kind of frustration which is likely to express itself in terms of active aggression against those responsible for setting the challenge.

That seems to be precisely what happened in the case of Jesus himself, whose teaching not merely as expressed in words but as embodied in his life produced the strongest possible opposition from those best qualified to assess its implications. That he knew that this was bound to happen is evident from the Gospels themselves, and particularly, for example, from such passages as those in which 'he began to teach them [his disciples] that the Son of man must suffer many things, and be rejected by the elders, and the chief priests, and the scribes, and be killed and after three days rise again' (Mark viii. 31). In other words the description of Jesus as 'one of the great teachers of mankind for all time', while accurate so far as it goes, only really makes sense if it is understood in the perspective of the Cross and the Resurrection.   W.W.S.

This teaching was summarized more particularly in a series of isolated aphorisms, collected together in the New Testament and known as the Sermon on the Mount. Here Jesus drew an idealistic picture of man living in righteousness and showed how his way of life could be transformed so as to attain a condition of blessedness. For most of these sayings it is possible to find parallels scattered about the Old Testament or the Apocrypha or contemporary rabbinic literature. But taken together, and related to the life and general outlook of their author, they constituted something new and unsurpassed in the world's ethical teaching. This may be described, for want of better terms, as the dynamic of love.

Jesus, as we have seen, was of humble stock and knew from his early experience in Galilee the hearts of the poor and oppressed, of what today we should call the under-dog. This gave him an understanding of human trouble and exceptionally wide sympathies, wherein lay the secret of his personal magnetism. Taken in conjunction with his undeviating veneration of God, they gave rise to an attitude of extreme humility expressed again and again throughout the Beatitudes. There is a blessedness reserved for the meek, the mourners, the merciful and the persecuted, which the rich, the powerful and the arrogant will never know. Jesus taught men the virtues of forgiveness, of patience, of charity in thought and word as well as in deed. He warned them against hypocrisy and ostentation and spiritual pride which was, in his eyes, the deadliest of sins.

Certain specific vices he mentioned by name as fatal to man's moral nature. Among them were anger, lust and the habit of swearing by oath. His teaching about these is characteristic in its extremism, its reference to absolute principles. The man who is angry with his brother and calls him 'fool' is in danger of hell-fire. The adulterous man is 'every one that looketh on a woman to lust after her'. Swearing by oath is blasphemy. 'Let your speech be Yea, yea; Nay, nay.' That is, be strong enough to keep your word without invocation, which is a sign of moral weakness.

Jesus has often been called the first great pacifist, and there are certainly elements in his teaching (as there were in the case of Jeremiah) which lend colour to this view. The principle of non-resistance is affirmed many times in the Sermon on the Mount. It was not altogether a new one, as is clear from certain passages in the Old Testament which at least deprecate retaliation: 'If thine enemy be hungry, give him bread to eat; and if he be thirsty, give him water to drink' (Prov. xxv. 21). 'Thou shalt not abhor an Edomite [Israel's traditional foe]; for he is thy brother' (Deut. xxiii. 7). There are Talmudical sayings, too, which amplify this principle. But Jesus' teaching on the subject, as on so many others, was far more forthright than anything that had preceded it. He taught men that the dynamic of love was to apply even to their enemies, was indeed even more imperative in their case. If your enemy smites you on the right cheek, turn your left to him; if he steals your coat, give him your cloak. There is no merit in loving your friends; if you want to be the child of your Father in heaven, then: 'Love your enemies, do good to them that hate you, bless them that curse you, pray for them that despitefully use you' (Luke vi. 27–28).

Here is plain enough advocacy of the principle of non-violence, stated in unequivocal terms, and it is further reinforced by Jesus' final warning to his disciples: 'All they that take the sword shall perish with the sword.' Right up to the present day men have quoted Jesus, and justifiably so, when they refused to take part in war on conscientious grounds. Yet it would be a mistake to think that throughout his life he acted consistently in accordance with this doctrine. There were moments when he was not averse to the use of violence, as when he forcibly cleared the Temple of money-changers or when, if we are to believe Luke, he contemplated armed resistance at Gethsemane. There was further the statement: 'Think not that I came to send peace on the earth: I came not to send peace, but a sword.' This in the context implied that the message he proclaimed would inevitably produce conflict both within and among human beings (Matt. x. 34).

The two sayings about the sword mentioned above seem to me to provide perfect examples of the 'speaking in hyperbole and paradox' to which Polack refers. Thus it is possible to interpret the curious reference to selling a cloak and buying a sword in Luke xxii. 35 f. as if Jesus were suggesting to his followers that if they were thinking of defending themselves and their cause by force they would need to sell the very clothes they wore in order to buy a sword, which is just another way of pointing out the futility of such defence. Their reply, 'Lord, here are two swords', would then be just another example of the characteristic failure even of those nearest to him to see the meaning, not merely of what he was saying to them but also of the situation in which they actually found themselves. His own comment, 'It is enough', might then be interpreted as meaning that there was no more to be said. 'If you haven't understood, what is the point of pursuing the matter further?' The real point surely is that the situation was quite beyond their capacity to understand.

The second statement about sending 'not peace, but a sword' is, I think, simply a vivid and forceful way of stating what I have tried to convey in a previous note, namely that when an individual (or for that matter a community) takes seriously the teaching and example of Jesus, some crisis is bound to follow. Again, it is only in the perspective of what was involved in his death and resurrection that the crisis can be resolved.   W.W.S.

The truth is that it is always difficult to draw precise rulings on contemporary moral problems from Jesus' teaching. He was apt to speak in metaphor, hyperbole and paradox, and he was addressing the simple folk of his own age and country in the rhetorical idiom which was most likely to appeal to them. Further, the strength of the moral dilemma with which he was constantly confronted, as is exemplified by the story of the Temptation, and his inner conviction about the imminence of the kingdom enabled him to live, as it were, at two levels at the same or successive moments. Hence we have the contradiction in his teaching already noticed, and it would be a fatal mistake to think of him in academic terms as the compiler of a code of ethics like some of the Talmudical Rabbis whose 'responsa' could be accorded a kind of judical validity. He spoke, as he thought, from the heart, and his pronouncements, based on first principles, often had little relation to the practical, worldly world as we know it.

This transcendental approach, if we may call it so, led him to express extremist views on many of the institutions and practices which govern the organized life of a community. Celibacy, for instance, he appears to have regarded as a more blessed state than marriage. When marriage took place, it was to be an indissoluble union of man and woman ordained by God from the beginning of the creation. 'They are no more twain, but one flesh', and therefore no cause is serious enough for them to be parted. 'What therefore God hath joined together, let not man put asunder.' If, as is unlikely, he revised this view at a later day it was to follow the strict ruling of the School of Shammai which, in opposition to the gentle Hillel, allowed divorce only in the case of a wife who had committed adultery.

I wonder whether it is really fair to suggest that Jesus regarded celibacy 'as a more blessed state than matrimony'. I agree that he himself remained celibate, but I cannot find in his teaching anything to suggest that he disapproved of others marrying. Nor is it without significance that the order of service for the solemnization of matrimony in the Book of Common Prayer refers to the institution, in its opening paragraph, as 'an holy estate which Christ adorned and beautified with his presence and first miracle that he wrought in Cana of Galilee'. It is, after all, to St. Paul and not to Jesus that we owe the seemingly reluctant concession that 'it is better to marry than to burn'.
                                                                                        W.W.S.

Again, on the subject of property many of his utterances (especially those quoted in Luke) seem to show that he held the communistic view of the contemporary Essenes. His hatred of wealth and the power that comes from possessions led him to glorify the poor, the abject, the disinherited. If a man wanted to attain to the condition of blessedness, he must give away everything that he had and live like the raven or the lily of the field, without toil or anxiety or any thought of material welfare. 'It is easier for a camel to go through a needle's eye, than for a rich man to enter into the kingdom of God' (Matt. xix. 24).

This extremist and uncompromising doctrine of salvation is exemplified elsewhere in Jesus' teaching. His knowledge of the weakness and sinfulness of human nature, coupled with his lofty conception of what was required in the way of conduct by God, led him at times into a feeling of utter hopelessness about man as a creature almost irretrievably lost. There was a perpetual conflict within him between the great love and tender sympathy he felt for his fellow-creatures and this strong conviction that the wicked, who were in the vast majority, must be consumed before the world could win salvation. We have perhaps here an echo of the old Prophetic teaching that Israel would be saved by a faithful remnant. But both the Rabbis and Jesus applied this to the individualist ethic, and their moral exclusiveness sometimes led them into what has been called 'the odious doctrine of the many who will be lost and of the few who will be "saved" '. 'For narrow is the gate, and straitened the way, that leadeth unto life, and few be they that find it' (Matt. vii. 14). Such sayings are disturbing to our modern ideas of humanitarianism; but once again we must remember the age in which they were uttered, the expectancy of an immediate 'day of judgment', and the consequent tendency to speak in absolute terms.

As against these limitations and contradictions in Jesus' teaching with regard to specific human institutions and current moral practice must be set the general tone and quality of his pleading, of his emotional appeal to the hearts of men. It is this that makes him pre-eminent among the teachers of the world. He saw everywhere that man's actions were governed by self-interest, by the half-truths of sophistry and legalism, by 'semblance of worth, not substance'. He carried on an unending campaign against self-deception, sham and hypocrisy. He implored men to look deep into their hearts and examine their motives on the basis of first principles. He set before them in a new, positive form the dynamic of love as a touchstone for all their actions.

In the fierce glare of such an illumination most of their impulses and reactions became irrelevant. They were shown to be shallow, self-centred and acquisitive. Jesus demanded a complete selflessness. A man must not consider himself, but only how he can serve

God and God's creatures. He must tend with loving care the poor, the sick, the 'lost sheep'. He must seek out the sinners and the disreputable and welcome them back to human society. He must pray for his enemies and repay hate with love. He must forgive those who have wronged him, and show no anger or resentment when he is reviled. Only an extreme humility and a boundless love could reconcile the envious and the vindictive, chasten the arrogant and self-important, and win the hard, cruel world for the service of God.

Through this pleading Jesus gave a sense of direction to the long line of workers and reformers, from his day to ours, who have set themselves to establish social righteousness among men. The germ of his teaching, as has been emphasized more than once, is to be found in the message of the Prophets and the ancient Hebrew sages and poets. But his direct appeal to the individual soul, and his formulation of an idealistic concept of ethical behaviour, gave a fresh and lasting impetus to all the subsequent regenerative movements of mankind.

It remains true, however, that no human being, not even Jesus himself, has been able to live up to this ideal. It is beyond the reach of natures that still retain some of the passions and appetites of their primitive state, and in which there is an instinctive urge towards self-preservation. In many ways Jesus did, indeed, attain to his ideal of self-mastery and resignation. He gave up all private pleasures in order to minister to the poor and suffering and preach to sinful men the word of God. He renounced private property and the joys of family life. He did not marry and have children. He consorted with the lowest and the most despised of his country-men and gave them new hope. He could even rise to the great height of praying for his persecutors: 'Father, forgive them; for they know not what they do.'

But confronted with the greatest test of all he fell short, as all noble men must who aspire beyond the limits that their human state has imposed on them. The sin that he hated most in man was self-righteousness and spiritual arrogance. Yet one may find traces of this in his own character. He could forgive men their wickedness and folly, all the carnal vices that flesh is heir to, even their brutality towards himself. But he could not forgive those who thought that God was on their side, who opposed him and his teaching in the name of religion. These appeared to stultify his whole life and outlook. Many of them were religious pedants who stuck to the letter of the law and forgot its spirit, who, as we have seen, made a parade of their piety and yet stole the widows' mites. These we should have expected Jesus to reprove, but with love and forbearance in his heart, and to pray for in the spirit of his great sermon. Yet though on occasion he had friendly social relations with individuals, there is no trace of any tenderness towards them as a group. 'Judge not, that ye be not judged', was what he preached; yet he branded the whole order of Scribes and Pharisees as 'serpents' and 'offspring of vipers' and consigned them to 'the judgment of hell'. He seems at times to have forgotten their common humanity, that they, too, were children of God – a thing he never did in the case of other sinners. Nor, as far as we know, did he attempt, by a kindly word or deed, to win them over to his point of view. Like the ancient Hebrew Prophets when dealing with the wicked or the enemies of Israel, he confined himself to the language of bitter denunciation.

It is possible that the evangelist, writing amid the stress of early Christian-Jewish conflicts, has put more into his mouth than he intended, but many have felt that there was here some gap in Jesus' spiritual armour. To the greatest excellence of all, it seems, even Jesus could not aspire; for this is beyond the grasp of mortal man. His failure in this one respect only serves to throw into relief the loftiness of his general aim and conduct. It can be accounted for in two ways, of which one, his attitude towards ceremonial religion and morality based on convention, forms the subject of the following chapter.

The other, which may be called the psychological cause, is to be found in Jesus' emotional nature. We have seen in previous chapters how, on occasion, he was wounded and cut to the heart by opposition and misrepresentation. This could reduce him to moods of depression and despair. Like his great forerunner, Jeremiah, to whom he bears so marked a resemblance, he had always to contend with an inner lack of confidence and a deep sensitiveness of the soul. But this did not cause him to shrink from living dangerously. For allied to it was its counterpart – a natural buoyancy, a forthrightness, a welling enthusiasm which rested upon infinite trust in God and was able to surmount and overwhelm every impediment with which his adventurous course confronted him.

The opposition of the Pharisees struck his ardent nature at its tenderest point. He looked to them for support, for he was of their order, and found many of them coldly critical and hostile. It was a blow to his *amour propre*, for no man felt what Virgil called *mens sibi conscia recti* – a mind conscious within itself of right – more acutely or more whole-heartedly than he did. And so there was this outburst of mortification, this one serious failure to live up to his own ideal. Yet the ideal remains a permanent goal towards which the spiritual nature of man perpetually strives. And its creator was the great ethical teacher who made 'impossible demands' which he himself just failed to fulfil, but in such a way that he compelled men to 'will the possible more strongly than before'.

It is in these last few paragraphs, I think, that we come to the point at which A.I.P.'s estimate of Jesus breaks down most seriously from the Christian point of view. I should not myself be prepared to defend any purely mechanical doctrine of the absolute perfection of Jesus, for that, I believe, would be to limit the reality of the Incarnation itself. For it is of the very essence of the Christian doctrine of the Incarnation that it involved the acceptance by Christ himself of certain limitations. But I should find it difficult to accept the suggestion that those limitations included any tendencies on his part to self-righteousness and spiritual arrogance. Nor can I believe that they included the kind of limitations to his understanding of men that seems to be implied by A.I.P.'s assessment of his attitude to the 'religious pedants who stuck to the letter of the law and forgot its spirit'. There is no reason to suppose that he did not 'pray for them in the spirit of his great sermon', but it is the peculiar tragedy of the particular sin of which they were guilty – or of the disease from which they were suffering – that it places the sinner beyond the reach of any normal reproach. Its most characteristic symptoms are spiritual blindness and deafness, symptoms which call for the use of shock tactics. But, as I have already suggested in an earlier note, the shock tactics that are appropriate to this particular spiritual condition are likely to have very disturbing consequences. We do not like to be confronted with our unconscious motives of greed and selfishness and pride, and the normal reaction is inevitably one of strong aggression towards the person who, whether by word or deed, and whether intentionally or unintentionally, is responsible for bringing about such a confrontation.

In the case of Jesus and those of his contemporaries who had allowed themselves to become so preoccupied with the externals of religion as almost to lose sight of the spirit, it has always seemed to me that he knew precisely what he was doing when he used the methods he did to stab them awake to the reality of their situation. He knew also what must be the inevitable consequences of his action. The conspiracy which encompassed his death was no surprise to him. Indeed, it might well be said that he knowingly provoked it, believing as he did that only his *acceptance of the consequences of* their *hardness of heart would bring about their eventual liberation.*

For this reason I find A.I.P.'s concluding paragraphs, in which he represents Jesus as 'wounded and cut to the heart by opposition and misrepresentation', strangely unsatisfying. While I appreciate to the full the sincerity and sympathy with which they are written, and while I would not for a moment minimize the cost to Jesus himself of all that he endured, I cannot believe that he went to the Cross in any other way than with his eyes wide open as to what it was that he was doing – and why. In the presence of that profound mystery it is surely not for us to sympathize with him but, rather, to remember his words to 'the great multitude of the people and of women who bewailed and lamented him' when, on his way to be crucified, he said: 'Daughters of Jerusalem, weep not for me, but weep for yourselves and for your children.' W.W.S.

CHAPTER XI

TEACHINGS: III. PRACTICAL

THE eternal paradox in Jesus' teaching is nowhere better illustrated than in his attitude to the ceremonial law. On the one hand, in all its essentials he lived the life of a Pharisaic Jew. He never attacked the Torah as a whole or himself laid down any principles which were contrary to Halachic teaching. His actual claim was that he came to fulfil the Law and not to destroy it. Yet in spite of this, as we saw in the last chapter, he found himself in violent conflict with the very party whose function it was to safeguard the sacred tradition and which based its life on adherence to its minutest requirements. And on occasion he did not scruple himself to set it aside when he thought that something more vital was at stake.

That Jesus assumed the validity of the Mosaic code and its current interpretation on the basis of the oral law is clear from what he did not say as much as from what he did. There are whole aspects of Jewish teaching and practice on which he does not comment and of which his approval may be taken for granted. Judaism was (and still is) a practical religion aimed at showing man the way to live a saintly life in accordance with the will of God. It was not much given to metaphysical or mystical speculation. Rather, it laid down statutes and judgments 'which if a man do, he shall live in them'. No clear distinction (in spite of some Prophetic criticism) was drawn between ceremonial performance and moral conduct. It hallowed every act and moment of a man's life, his waking and sleeping, his taking of meals, his study and his daily round of work. In all this Jesus was brought up from childhood, and it was a way of life which must have appealed in a special degree to his deeply spiritual and impressionable nature.

There is abundant evidence, too, that he applied these principles of Halachic law to his own teaching and practice. When a man had been cleansed from leprosy he ordered him to show himself to the priest and bring the customary offering to the Temple. A man who had quarrelled with his neighbour was to become reconciled with him before offering a gift at the altar. He put on *tephillin*, went up to Jerusalem for the Feast of Passover, and observed the ritual of Seder night. When he opposed divorce, he was careful not to attack the law of Moses. His explanation – 'For your hardness of heart he wrote you this commandment' – shows that he looked upon it with respect. The prayer which he taught his disciples, 'Our Father, which art in heaven', is an anthology of devotional language drawn from both the Old Testament and rabbinic writings.

It was, in fact, his constant habit to appeal to the Old Testament when questioned on points of conduct. When a man asked him how he could inherit eternal life, he replied: 'Thou shalt not kill, Thou shalt not commit adultery, Thou shalt not steal, Thou shalt not bear false witness, Honour thy father and thy mother' (Matt. xix. 18–19). This is an almost exact replica of the last section of the Ten Commandments. When the man said, 'All these things have I observed from my youth', Jesus 'looking upon him loved him'. And again, when he was asked by one of the Scribes which he considered the most important of all the Commandments, he answered just as a contemporary Rabbi such as Hillel might have answered: 'The first is, Hear, O Israel; the Lord our God, the Lord is one: and thou shalt love the Lord thy God with all thy heart, and with all thy soul, and with all thy mind, and with all thy strength. The second is this, Thou shalt love thy neighbour as thyself. There is none other commandment greater than these' (Mark xii. 29–31). And to the Scribe, who thereupon accepted this pronouncement, he addressed these words: 'Thou art not far from the kingdom of God.'

For it must be borne in mind that, even in his denunciations of the hypocritical Pharisees, about which we read in the last chapter, Jesus was not speaking very differently from the Rabbis themselves. The 'woes' were actually introduced by a general endorsement of their order. 'The scribes and the Pharisees sit on Moses' seat: all things therefore whatsoever they bid you, these do and observe.' In his subsequent attack on their ostentation, hypocrisy and externalism he was echoing a great deal that they themselves were saying about the least reputable members of their own sect. These are referred to in the Talmud as the 'Pharisaic plague', 'the dyed ones', 'those who preach beautifully, but do not act beautifully'. It was only in his indiscriminate condemnation of the whole order

that Jesus seems to have departed from normal Pharisaic precedent, and one wonders how much of this was put into his mouth by
the evangelist who wrote at a time when the new Church was
struggling to emancipate itself from traditional Judaism. For even
in the violence of his invective Jesus gave support by implication
to the upholding of the ceremonial law: 'Woe unto you, Pharisees!
for ye tithe mint and rue and every herb, and pass over judgment
and the love of God: but these *ought ye to have done*, and not to
leave the other undone' (Luke xi. 42).

Yet there were moments in the life of this Pharisaic Jew when
he did seem to question the relevance of Torah to the new age that
was now fast approaching. Two statements in particular were
taken by the later Church to signify that he regarded his own
coming as the supersession of traditional Judaism. One (quoted
somewhat differently in Matthew) ran as follows: 'The law and the
prophets were until John: from that time the gospel of the kingdom of God is preached, and every man entereth violently unto it.'
Even here Luke (xvi. 17) adds: 'But it is easier for heaven and
earth to pass away, than for one tittle of the Law to fall.' The
second, from Mark ii. 21–22, is a protest against religious compromise, against the view that it is possible to graft the new faith
on the old. 'No man seweth a piece of undressed cloth on an old
garment: else that which should fill it up taketh from it, the new
from the old, and a worse rent is made. And no man putteth new
wine into old wine-skins: else the wine will burst the skins, and
the wine perisheth, and the skins: but they put new wine into fresh
wine-skins.'

These passages would seem to imply that Jesus desired a fundamental break with the past and was sceptical about the possibility
of gradual change or reform. This attitude was, in effect, a criticism of the whole rabbinic method whereby those enactments of
the ancient code which had become obsolete were modified by
fresh interpretation and legal fiction. Any kind of half-heartedness
was, indeed, antipathetic to his enthusiastic nature and sense of
urgency, and nothing was more repugnant to him than a quibbling,
legalistic approach to moral problems.

Apart from these general statements, there were occasions in
his life when he showed both in word and deed his impatience of
certain particular formalities and restrictions imposed by Torah.
His disciples were allowed to break the regulations concerning the

Sabbath (though not its spirit) when they picked ears of corn to satisfy their hunger as they passed through a field. He was ready to heal the sick man on the Sabbath even though his life was not in danger. The ritual washing of the hands before meals was on occasion neglected; Jesus was more interested in moral cleansing and the purification of the heart. In particular he offended the Pharisees by his attitude towards the laws of separation. These made a clear distinction between the 'clean' and the 'unclean', and the former would not be allowed by a strict interpretation of the code to consort with the latter. Jesus set these regulations aside and sat down to eat with 'publicans and sinners'. Even harlots he treated as human beings. There were also his specific pronouncements on Corban, the importance of oaths and the dietary laws: 'Not that which entereth into the mouth defileth the man; but that which proceedeth out of the mouth, this defileth the man' – which seemed to be in direct contravention of the Law.

For these reasons it appeared to the Pharisees that Jesus was deliberately encouraging sinners. As has been explained, the ceremonial regulations were in their eyes inextricably bound up with morality and good social behaviour. You could not defy the one without seriously imperilling the other. And there was this to be said on their behalf, that a strict adherence to Halachic principles would in fact ensure the leading of an upright and saintly life.

But, as so often happens with a code which attempts to embody their highest aspirations in a set of legal forms, men in their weakness tend to forget the inner spirit in their eagerness for outward conformity; the latter has the constant glare of publicity. Jesus must have seen this frequent breakdown in practice and, with his penetrating insight and tendency to refer all human conduct to first principles, he came at times to the conclusion that 'the letter killeth'. There were so many contingencies in which scrupulous obedience to the code seemed to him to lead men into uncharitable conduct towards their fellows and make them lose sight of their simple common humanity. That is one reason which accounts for the apparent discrepancy in Jesus' attitude towards the ceremonial law. On the one hand, he thought of it as the instrument of an upright life and the outward expression of all that was best in the Judaism in which he was reared; it was never, therefore, his explicit object to abolish it. On the other hand, he saw it acting on occasion as a barrier to the attainment of that inner kingdom of God which required no ceremonial forms, but demanded from men the perfect life, 'as your heavenly Father is perfect'. Thus we have no artificial antithesis in the mind of Jesus. It was just the recognition of the gulf which always exists between promise and performance, of which the best minds in all religious groups are painfully aware. So much, indeed, he shared with the genuinely pious among the Pharisees.

But there was a further element in his teaching, already noted in the chapter on ethics, which made him in a sense a rebel against all society as such and led him to attack, either directly or by implication, the whole framework of ceremonies and conventions by which groups of men bind themselves together. In his concentration on the perfecting of the individual human soul he seemed to ignore the claims made on man by his very membership of a community. His feeling that ordered, settled life, as it was known up till that time, was facing catastrophe, was about to be overwhelmed in a sudden and violent manner, induced in him a profound distrust of all human societies and institutions. He never joined any of the many parties or groups, such as the Zealots or Essenes, which aimed at some practical solution of contemporary problems. He was uninterested in the claims of patriotism, civil justice, national culture or organized reform. His purpose was far other than the creation of a welfare state.

It is easy to see that in this he parted company with all except a small group of dreamers, called for convenience the Apocalyptic Pharisees. The official Pharisees were *par excellence* the upholders of custom and convention. The Essenes bound themselves by an elaborate code of obligations and vows. The Sadducees stood for hierarchical prestige and the maintenance of the Temple ritual. The Zealots were united in their determination to set Israel free by the practical application of force. None of these ways appealed to the intuitive mind of Jesus, for they had no bearing on the genuine crisis which he saw as threatening the whole human race.

In rejecting them it is sometimes thought that he made a special point of rejecting the Jewish people as such, and that he looked to the Gentiles or some new association of men to carry out his work. There are, indeed, one or two passages in the Synoptic Gospels which on a superficial reading might lend colour to this view. Notable among these are the 'woes' he pro-

nounced against the cities of Galilee: 'It shall be more tolerable for
Tyre and Sidon in the day of judgment, than for you'; and his
denunciation of Jerusalem: 'O Jerusalem, Jerusalem, which killeth
the prophets, and stoneth them that are sent unto her! how often
would I have gathered thy children together, even as a hen gathereth
her own brood under her wings, and ye would not!' And there is
the more explicit statement in a passage recorded by Luke
describing the difficulty of entering through the gate of heaven:
'There shall be the weeping and gnashing of teeth, when ye shall
see Abraham, and Isaac, and Jacob, and all the prophets, in the
kingdom of God, and yourselves cast forth without. And they shall
come from the east and west, and from the north and south, and
shall sit down in the kingdom of God.' (Matthew adds: 'but the
sons of the kingdom shall be cast forth into the outer darkness.')
Further, there are one or two parables, such as those of the great
feast and the vineyard, which might be taken to imply some special
rejection of the House of Israel.

But to draw this conclusion from these few selected passages is
to wrench them from their wider context. It was natural that Jesus,
in his indignation and grief over the wickedness of men's ways,
should attack the society in which he lived, indeed the only one
of which he had intimate knowledge. In this he was merely following the precedent set by the Hebrew prophets. There is no evidence that he preferred or commended the ways of other peoples,
such as the Romans or Phoenicians or Hellenistic Greeks, who
lived in and about the land of Israel at this time and with whom he
presumably came into contact. Moreover, the opposition he
encountered came inevitably from his fellow Jews, the vast
majority of whom rejected his special claims. It followed that the
emotional outbursts of his deeply sensitive and sorely wounded
nature would be directed against those of his own people who were
deaf to his appeal.

Nevertheless, it is clear from the whole tone and idiom of his
teaching that Jesus felt himself to be a Jew in every sense of the
word and accepted the traditional view that his nation had been
divinely chosen. He distinctly stated that he was 'not sent but
unto the lost sheep of the house of Israel'. He also instructed his
disciples not to go the way of the Gentiles, nor enter into any city
of the Samaritans, 'but go rather to the lost sheep of the house of
Israel'. On occasion his utterances would betray the normal feeling

of national superiority which belonged to ancient peoples – has it ceased today? – and he did not scruple to speak of other races with a certain contempt. 'As a Gentile and as a publican' was a phrase he used to express disdain. When asked by a Phoenician woman to cure her daughter, he replied: 'It is not meet to take the children's bread and cast it to the dogs.' In other words, 'my gifts of healing are not to be wasted on Gentiles'. It is true that humaner feelings prevailed and that he did later cure the girl, but the language of his first impetuous outburst is revealing. (See p. 88.) Even in his generous praise of the modest, tolerant centurion – 'I have not found so great faith, no, not in Israel' – he showed by implication where his first loyalties lay. Finally, when speaking of the right way to pray he warned his disciples not to use 'vain repetitions', as the Gentiles do, 'for they think that they shall be heard for their much speaking' (Matt. vi. 7).

We should be right, then, in concluding that Jesus rejected neither Judaism nor the Jewish people, and that he had even inherited a certain sense of national exclusiveness. But to think that his message could be defined or circumscribed in these terms would be a gross error of judgment and could only lead to a false assessment of the value of his teaching. We have noted earlier the inherent paradox in his attitude towards the ceremonial law. This would apply equally to his whole conception of morality and social life. His concentration on man as an individual with a personal relation to God led him far beyond the confines of nationality and even the holiest of religious systems. This is shown not so much by his occasional references to non-Israelites, to good Samaritans or Roman centurions, as by his constant appeal to men to ignore the conventions of the society in which they live and make themselves perfect with their Maker. From ancient times the Prophets and singers of Israel had made the same kind of appeal: 'O ye sons of men, how long shall my glory be turned into dishonour? How long will ye love vanity, and seek after falsehood? But know that *the Lord hath set apart him that is godly for himself*' (Ps. iv. 2–3). In his own time, too, the Rabbis, or the best of them, were exemplifying in their conduct the saintly way of life. But all alike thought of the individual, whatever the personal claims made on him by Kedushah or holiness, as part of society, and their bright visions of the future had a communal and often a markedly national setting.

Now all forms of human society are based on compromise. Some workable arrangement must be found in this imperfect world which balances the interests of the whole community with the claims of each individual soul. Too often in history this adjustment has been found at the lowest level of expediency, and much of the world's failure is directly attributable to this fact. There is no reason to suppose that the age in which Jesus lived was more wicked than any other. But perhaps the people by whom he was taught made higher pretensions to godliness than is usual, and their comparative failure to achieve the standards they set themselves led them into correspondingly more pronounced forms of complacency and pretence.

In any case Jesus, in his more inspired moments, would have nothing to do with compromise of any kind. His philosophy was a perfectionist philosophy and he was interested only in the absolute purity of the soul. In such moods he cared nothing about social structures or national stability. All settled, organized forms of life were based on self-interest and aimed at self-preservation. They led in practice to those adjustments and pretences and expedients which were most repugnant to his flaming sincerity and the most serious obstacles to his demand for absolute righteousness.

It was not surprising, therefore, that he came into open conflict with those whose function it was to uphold conventional morality. For their main concern was the preservation of the life and standards of the people through traditional forms and institutions. Jesus seemed to them to set all these at defiance. He was comparatively uninterested in the material or cultural life of the nation. He laid little stress on institutions such as marriage, the family, the possession of property, or the process of law by which it is secured. He seemed to them a subverter of society and a nihilist.

In this dispute, it was, as so often, a case of both sides being right. There were all the elements of a tragic conflict and one can well imagine Jesus protesting to his rabbinic opponents in the words used by Antigone to Creon:

> I did not think your edicts strong enough
> To overrule the unwritten, unalterable laws
> Of God and heaven . . .

The Pharisees were right in maintaining that man is a 'social animal', and that if any human society is to be preserved it must be through the medium of its culture, that is, by means of customs, laws, contracts and economics. But Jesus was also right in proclaiming that man has an immortal soul whose allegiance is owed direct to its spiritual author, and that in comparison with this overwhelming obligation the requirements of man-made, time-serving institutions are of no account.

Yet the paradox in his teaching lay in the fact that he could never say this or act this quite consistently throughout his life. All the time he carried with him associations deriving from the past history of his people and his early environment. It was to his fellow Jews that he addressed himself and he naturally used their language and the idiom that they understood. He was brought up in their religion and way of life and he never cut himself adrift. Emotionally and intellectually he remained a Jew and, even when he attacked certain types among them, he employed a technique that was Hebraic and which had its roots in the message of Hebrew prophecy.

And so, as we have seen in his treatment of ethics, the great value of his teaching lay in this very inconsistency, that he was able to think on two levels at once and to bring the perfectionist outlook to bear on the moral problems of practical life. His transcendental vision was never escapist, as is so often the case with the pure mystic. He could teach and live the life of practical Judaism, observe its precepts and carry out its ceremonies. And at the same time he could show, again in an entirely Jewish way, how utterly inadequate all such man-made institutions and conventions were, and how specially irrelevant they had become with the advent of the kingdom of God.

I am so far in agreement with what A.I.P. has written in this chapter that further interruption seemed unnecessary. At least, it did until I came to the paragraph on p. 134 beginning: 'In any case, Jesus in his more inspired moments . . .' And there, I think, we come very near to the crux of the whole matter. For it is just here that, from the Christian point of view, even so utterly sincere and sympathetic an attempt as my colleague's to interpret Jesus in terms of being a great teacher breaks down.

He is, I think, quite right in suggesting that there is much in the teaching of Jesus that would justify our describing him as a 'perfectionist'. And a 'perfectionist' is always a problem. It is in no way sur-

prising that 'those whose function it was to uphold conventional morality' should have come to regard him as 'a subverter of society and a nihilist'. For the 'conventional moralist' is generally realist enough to recognize the limitations of human nature. He does not set a standard so high as to be virtually unattainable by men – as Jesus seems to have done. Here, then, is the dilemma. The conventional moralist sets a standard which is practicable but fundamentally unsatisfying – for there is an element of the perfectionist in most men. At heart we should all like to say 'yes' to the ideal. But in fact we are most of us compelled in the long run to acknowledge, however reluctantly, that 'human nature being what it is' the ideal is beyond our grasp. Instead of saying 'yes' we are driven in the last resort to a reluctant, a regretful, perhaps even a resentful, 'no'.

The reluctant are those who, unwilling to acknowledge their own limitations, fight on to the last ditch of moral rectitude without ever appearing to know, and certainly without ever being able to communicate to others, anything in the nature of true moral freedom. They become the slaves of an ideal, and even though they 'give their bodies to be burned' the sacrifice appears to lack the 'charity' that alone can give it real significance.

The regretful are those who, having shrugged their spiritual shoulders and admitted their limitations, settle down to the 'conventional morality' of those who are content to 'act' their way through life.

The resentful are those who are unwilling to accept the conventional, but are incapable of the sustained efforts of the idealists. In these, reluctance and regret turn sour and find aggressive outlet in the attempt to destroy the ideal itself. It is a nice point, worthy, I think, of very serious consideration, as to whether, in the long run, we do most of us find ourselves in this third group.

But in the meantime, what of Jesus himself? A.I.P. attempts to resolve the paradox thus inevitably created by suggesting that although Jesus 'was right in proclaiming that man has an immortal soul whose allegiance is owed direct to its spiritual author and that in comparison with this overwhelming obligation the requirements of man-made, time-serving institutions are of no account . . . he could never say or act quite consistently with this throughout his life'. It is necessary, therefore, according to this interpretation, to attribute to Jesus the ability 'to think on two levels at once'. And on these premises this is a perfectly sound and logical position to adopt.

The Christian, however, starts from other premises which, it should be clearly understood, were not apparent either to the supporters or the critics of Jesus during his lifetime. His earliest critics were the Pharisees who were best qualified to see the dilemma into which both his teaching and example were bound eventually to force any who gave allegiance to him. The last to abandon him were his disciples, most of them Galileans, who appear to have been drawn to him less by his teaching than by the force of his personality. Attached to him by the bonds of personal friendship, they clung desperately and to the last minute to the belief that they could do what he appeared to expect of them.

This is nowhere more vividly or forcefully presented than in the story of Peter on the night before the Crucifixion. In Mark xiv. 27 f. we find Peter assuring Jesus that 'although all shall be offended, yet will not I', and a moment later, with exceeding vehemence, affirming, 'If I must die with thee, I will not deny thee'. Yet it was only a very short while after, in the Garden of Gethsemane, that Jesus was asking Peter: 'Simon, sleepest thou? couldest thou not watch one hour?' And again, later the same night, we read in the same Gospel and chapter that in reply to the thrice repeated taunt of a servant-girl, Peter 'began to curse and to swear, I know not this man of whom ye speak'.

What, then, are we to make of Jesus who could force not only his opponents but also his friends into such an impossible situation? If he was simply the great teacher, reaffirming in word and example the great ideals of those who had gone before him in Israel and pushing those ideals to their logical conclusion, we are left simply with the tragic spectacle of yet another martyr to a high but hopeless cause. That indeed was all that his contemporaries – even his closest friends – could see in it, up to the moment of his dying.

But what seemed to so many the end proved for some to be but a new beginning. For, so the Christian believes, Jesus was not only 'crucified, dead and buried' but 'on the third day he rose again from the dead'. This is the premise which gives a new dimension to the whole. For instead of being left with the story of a perfectionist paying the price of his own fanaticism and leaving his friends and followers simply with a frustrating example to which in their heart of hearts they knew they could never hope to aspire, those to whom he appeared after his resurrection found themselves enlivened and uplifted by the continuing presence of one whom not even death itself could hold. And the only way in which they could make sense of what had happened was to assert, not that man had achieved divinity, but that God had in some mysterious and quite inexplicable way condescended to be made man.

I come back, then, to the point I have already made in several previous notes, that the ultimate question we have to face about Jesus has to do, not with the content of his teaching, nor with the way in which he performed his mighty works, but with what manner of man he was.

W.W.S.

CHAPTER XII

JESUS' SIGNIFICANCE IN WORLD HISTORY

WE have now completed a survey of the life and teaching of Jesus and are in a position to make some estimate of the man and the significance of his impact on history. The task is especially complicated for two reasons which have already been touched on in previous chapters. The first is the paucity of reliable material and contemporary evidence with regard to Jesus' life. The second lies in the accumulation of matter belonging to the sphere of metaphysics which grew up around him after his death and tended to obscure the original, historical personality. It was the product of those for whom he became the central figure of a new revelation and brought with it its counter-part, namely the distortions of those who rejected this claim and continued to uphold their ancestral faith. The latter, as we have seen, felt themselves threatened by the growing influence of Christianity and, largely as the result of persecution, did their best to discredit and denigrate the character of its founder (see Chapter V).

Here I feel I must insert a mild caveat. That there is a paucity of 'reliable material and contemporary evidence' in the sense of independent, objective and scientific historical material I entirely agree. But these are not the only criteria of reliability, and I am sure A.I.P. would not wish to be interpreted as impugning the reliability of the Gospels. He would, I think, agree that they represent the perfectly genuine and sincere attempts of men whose lives had been turned upside down by their association with Jesus of Nazareth to explain what it was that had happened to them.

By the same token I should argue, as a Christian, that the 'accumulation of matter belonging to the sphere of metaphysics which grew up after his death' was not simply confusing the issues but was rather helping to clarify them for those who had found it impossible to understand or to explain Jesus in terms of any of the normal categories.

W.W.S.

In the case of Jesus we are often able to trace the exact sources of the many supernatural claims which later writers made about him when they sought for their own religious ideas 'a local habitation and a name'. It was said that he was 'born of a virgin', and this belief was based on a verse in Isaiah (vii. 14), though the Hebrew word in its context really meant 'young married woman'. The birth was placed at Bethlehem in order to fulfil, many scholars hold, a prophecy in Micah (v. 2). The story of the flight to Egypt probably arose from a passage in Hosea (xi. 1); that of Herod's supposed massacre of the Innocents from Jeremiah (xxxi. 15).

This is not the place, I think, to attempt any discussion of the problem of the Virgin Birth. I cannot, however, resist the temptation to point out what seems to me to be something of a non sequitur in A.I.P.'s argument in this paragraph. Belief in the virgin birth, he says, was based on Isaiah vii. 14: 'Behold a virgin shall conceive and bear a son. . . .' But if, as he insists, the Hebrew word 'almah' in this context really meant 'young married woman' it is perhaps a little surprising that the idea of a virgin birth should have been derived from it. More probable, I should have thought, was that the verse from Isaiah was adduced in support of a belief that had already begun to gain currency. The Hebrew word in question means quite simply a young woman who is sexually mature. It is quite indeterminate as to whether she is married or not, and although A.I.P. may be right in assuming that in this context it is to be understood as meaning a young married woman there is no reason why it should not be translated as 'virgin'.
W.W.S.

Of the attitude of the Gospel writers a further word of explanation is required. They lived at a time when the new creed was struggling for its existence and had not yet completely emancipated itself from the old. It was their object to show that the coming of Jesus was the fulfilment of Old Testament prophecy and that his life and personality exactly fitted into the Apocalyptic picture. They therefore made use of a number of passages in this literature which foretold the coming of some great, and possibly supernatural, figure who, as God's messenger, would bring redemption to mankind. Similar treatment had been accorded to many of Israel's ancient heroes, such as Moses who, according to the Torah, received two tablets of stone from God himself on Mount Sinai,

or Elijah who was said to have been taken up to heaven in a
chariot of fire. Indeed it is a common feature of the stories of
ancient law givers and founders of religion that they tend to
magnify and, as Thucydides says, 'enthrone in the region of
legend' the personality of the hero and draw freely on current
belief and fancy.

*It is not really necessary, I think, to suggest parallels with other
stories of ancient law-givers and founders of religion. What the Gospel
writers were doing was only what rabbinic writers were constantly
doing, and their methods of handling and interpreting what for them
were the only authoritative scriptures they knew were entirely in
accordance with those traditionally employed by the Rabbis. Difficulties arose, however, when the interpretation or application of these
passages from the Hebrew Bible came to be vested with an authority
comparable with that of the original.*   W.W.S.

There remains the account of Jesus' bodily resurrection, im-
plicitly believed by the Gospel writers and later incorporated as a
fundamental article in the Christian faith. It was said that on the
third day after his death his tomb was found to be open and empty;
that it was guarded by angels in white apparel; that his risen body
was seen by his disciples and others on the road to Emmaus, in
Jerusalem itself and later in Galilee; that he took food with them
and declared that his spirit would return to them, and that after
'forty days' he was taken up to heaven. Finally his promise that
the Holy Spirit would manifest itself to them was, according to the
account in the Acts, fulfilled with a sound of 'a rushing mighty
wind' on the Feast of Pentecost, fifty days after his death.

Now it cannot be doubted that the origin of the resurrection
story is to be found in the actual experience of the immediate
followers of Jesus and their successors. So profound an impression
had been made upon them by his personality and spiritual power
that they could not regard the crucifixion as marking any final
severance. They felt his presence was still with them and, believing
in the doctrine of personal resurrection, they conceived of it in
physical terms. However subjective these visions might be, they
were none the less real to their beholders.

*Here again it will hardly surprise our readers to know that much as I
admire the sincerity of A.I.P.'s attempt to explain something which,*

ex hypothesi, *he cannot accept – in this case the story of the bodily resurrection of Jesus – I myself find his explanation completely unsatisfying. To base so fundamental a teaching of the Church upon the 'subjective visions' of the earliest disciples and 'the fertile ingenuity and fiery enthusiasm' of Paul of Tarsus seems to me to do far less than justice to the extraordinary way in which the New Testament writers themselves deal with this very difficult issue. For there is a* naïveté *and even inconsistency about some of the Gospel records of the Resurrection which, as it has always seemed to me, lends them a much more convincing air of verisimilitude than if they had been 'written up', however sincerely, to lend support to an already developed doctrine.*

W.W.S.

That the same belief about Jesus came to be accepted by the wider circle of Christians in subsequent generations, and was eventually incorporated in official Church doctrine, has a further explanation. During the formative years, and especially after the fall of Jerusalem, the new faith made little impact on the Jews of Palestine and won most of its adherents in the cities of the Roman-Hellenistic world. Here there were elements, both Jewish (often of Gentile extraction and recently converted) as well as pagan, ready to accept a new religion which was universalistic in conception and promised them personal salvation based on a high standard of human conduct.

It was to a large extent due to the fertile ingenuity and fiery enthusiasm of Paul of Tarsus that the new movement gradually spread among these elements until it finally became the dominant creed of the Roman Empire. Paul himself was a Hellenized Jew who knew both his Judaism and the religions and superstitions of the people amongst whom he lived. His intellectual dexterity enabled him to offer the pagan world a form of Judaism expressed in the idiom with which they were familiar. This meant, in effect, that he had to come to terms with the so-called mystery religions. These, as we have seen in a previous chapter, had a peculiar attraction for the peoples of the Graeco-Roman world. They offered at once an escape from the crudities of a state-controlled hierarchical cult and an opportunity for self-purification and mystical experience. They had many forms and exceedingly ancient origins. In the Greek world there was the cult of Orphism associated with the worship of Dionysus, the god of wine and passion, which arose as early as the sixth century B.C. and had its influence on Pythagoras and even Plato. There were the Eleusinian mysteries which celebrated the annual rebirth of Persephone (the daughter of Demeter, goddess of the corn-crop), symbolizing the earth's fertility. There was the drama of Prometheus, a god chained to the rock as a punishment for his friendship with man. There were the rites of Cybele and Attis, imported to Rome from Phrygia with great solemnity after the Punic wars. From Egypt came the worship of Isis and Osiris, as well as the deification of a Spartan king, Cleomenes III, after his crucifixion at Alexandria. From Persia arose the most potent rival of the new Christian faith, Mithraism.

Most of these had a certain basic element in common. They were dramas of life and death and rebirth. Primitive peoples were dominated by fear and superstition and regarded their world as the plaything of inscrutable and utterly irrational forces. These they sought by all their imaginative skill and fancy to make friendly and harness to their needs. In particular, their minds were obsessed by the mystery of death and, like many of their more rational successors, they longed to penetrate into the realm of the unknown and secure for themselves some kind of personal immortality. The mystery religion supplied this very need. It postulated some lord of the cult, Dionysus or Mithra it might be, whose transcendent power could reanimate the souls of those who believed in him and carried out the appropriate ritual. This generally consisted of some kind of personal identification with the deity concerned. It could be done through the process of sympathetic magic, when the initiate would himself re-enact the crucial drama of the life of his lord. Or salvation could be won through sacrifice. In this case the worshipper gained a mystical identification by being drenched with the blood of the particular animal that was sacred to his patron deity.

Besides the mystery religions there was, as we have seen, another way in which the world of Jesus' time attempted to bridge the gap between the remote and inscrutable mind of Providence and the dire needs and hopes of powerless humanity. This was a more intellectual approach to the problem and postulated the existence of some kind of an intermediary. In ancient Hebrew thought there had grown up the conception of Shechinah, a divine presence which shed its radiance on the Temple and was even transplanted to foreign lands when Israel went into exile. We also find such phrases as 'the voice of the Lord', 'the finger of God' used in the Old Testament, which were often more than metaphors and implied to the writers some anthropomorphic manifestation. This current of belief became crystallized in the personification of Wisdom (see p. 37) and in the Logos doctrine, derived from Heracleitus and Greek philosophy, which found its most complete expression in the writings of Philo and the Fourth Gospel. In their thought the universal, transcendental deity infused his spirit into the world of men, offering them a principle of wisdom and order and creativity on which human life could be based.

It is easy to see how much influence these ideas of the Graeco-Roman world have exerted on Christian theology. The root doctrines both of the Incarnation and Resurrection have been closely influenced by them. So has the Pauline teaching about Jesus as mediator and agent of salvation. They found their way into the Sacraments, such as the Mass (an adaptation of the Jewish Kiddush) whereby the initiate 'was fulfilled with the body and blood of his Saviour'. The purely Jewish traditional beliefs in the coming of a personal Messiah, the anointed servant of God, were thus grafted on to the mystical and intellectual conceptions of the world of Paul's experience. But all this could not have come about without the impact of Jesus' distinctive personality and genius on his own immediate environment.

Here again I feel a caveat is necessary, for while it was very fashionable some few years ago to lay great stress on the influence of these contemporary mystery religions on the development of Christian doctrine, New Testament scholars nowadays are much more inclined to look for – and indeed to find – the roots of those doctrines in Hebraic rather than in Hellenistic soil. This is not to rule out altogether the possibility of Hellenistic influence, but to speak, as A.I.P. does, of grafting 'the purely Jewish traditional beliefs . . . on to the mystical and intellectual conceptions of the world of Paul's experience' would seem to many people today to be describing the process in exact reverse. If there was any grafting it is much more likely to have been the grafting of Hellenistic ideas on to a Hebraic stock.   W.W.S.

It is true that Jesus himself never taught these doctrines or thought in these terms. He was both in practice and outlook a Pharisaic Jew whose conception of life was inherited from the

Rabbis and ancient Hebrew Prophets. He knew nothing of the occult mystery religions; Greek intellectualism and Logos-incarnation theories were remote from his experience. Nothing indeed would have surprised him more than to discover that he had become identified with the exotic ideas and practices of the non-Hebraic world.

Yet there were some aspects of his life and teaching that made this transition possible, and it is safe to say that such a metamorphosis could have taken place in the case of no other man, certainly no other Hebrew. First, as we have seen, some of his remarks lent colour to the view that he had come to inaugurate a new faith and that there must be an absolute break with the past. The essence of this faith was an absolute surrender on the part of its adherents to himself and his own direction. In comparison adherence to the ceremonial law was of minor importance. Salvation could be won only through his personal mediation. This gave Paul some grounds for a critical attitude towards the Law and for postulating the way of Christian salvation. It immediately appealed to the followers of the mystery cults who sought purification of the spirit through complete identification with the life of the patron deity.

Paul's attitude to the Law is another of the subjects which it is quite beyond the scope of these notes to discuss, but something at least must be said in favour of substituting the word 'paradoxical' for 'critical' in relation to it. For Paul, as a Jew, the Law remained what it had always been, 'holy and righteous and good'; and although as a Christian he describes its function as an educational one – it had been 'our schoolmaster to bring us to Christ' – there is nothing either derogatory or un-Jewish about that, for it has long been a rabbinic dictum that when Israel observes even one Sabbath perfectly (i.e. when Israel is perfectly obedient to the Law in only one of its aspects) the Messiah will come. Paul's criticism was directed not against the Law which, both as a Jew and as a Christian, he was content to accept as the inspired word of God, but against the weakness of his own, and indeed of all, human nature which, as I have mentioned in previous notes, assents in principle to an ideal to which in practice it proves itself incapable of attaining.   W.W.S.

Then again in much of his teaching Jesus seemed to imply a

special relationship with God. He never, it is true, claimed to be himself divine or a part of his heavenly Father, but he went far beyond the Prophets in asserting a special intimacy with God, in regarding himself as the selected instrument of a divine Providence – a role which the Prophets had reserved for the whole House of Israel. This was the essence of the Messianic conception, and it is easy to see how such teaching might lead to a belief in divine Sonship or the incarnation of the Logos, the 'Word of God', immanent in the physical life of man.

Our readers would hardly expect A.I.P. and myself to agree as to the significance of Jesus' teaching about his relationship with God. If we did we should be either both of us Jews or both of us Christians. I content myself, therefore, with saying that I think he seriously under-estimates the Messianic element both in the consciousness and in the teaching of Jesus. W.W.S.

More than all else, the manner of Jesus' death captured men's imagination and seemed in retrospect to have a symbolic, trans-cendental significance. Here was the fighter against evil, the champion of the oppressed, the messenger of God who had brought the 'good news', brutally sacrificed for the sins of mankind. Some words of his to his disciples during the last few days of his life, and especially at the Seder service, seemed to imply that in spite of his death his presence would always be with them, and that when he himself was no longer among them in the flesh a holy spirit would dwell with those who had faith in him and bring them continuing salvation. Thus was planted the germ of that belief in the threefold aspect of the divine which eventually took shape in Trinitarian doctrine.

It is clear, then, that any valuation of the significance of Jesus in world history must take into consideration first and foremost that he was the ultimate founder, the *causa causans*, of Christianity. Though in his life and thought he was a pure Jew, teaching and practising the religion of his fathers and knowing nothing of the mystical and Trinitarian theology of the later faith, nevertheless, by certain new emphases in his teaching, by his example of patient suffering, by the way in which he made the supreme sacrifice in defence of absolute principles, thereby seeming to have conquered death itself, he did in fact cause a small group of men to feel that they had received a new revelation and to think and act in such a way that they profoundly modified the whole subsequent course of history.

The more I read this paragraph – and I have read it many times – the more I feel that the only effective way of dealing with all the issues to which it gives rise would be to write another book! But since that, at least at this stage, is out of the question, I can only express the view that it provides a totally inadequate foundation for all that was to follow. For its logical implication is that what in fact can only be interpreted as a turning-point in history is based on the last analysis on the subjective fancy of a small group of Galilean peasants. W.W.S.

This does not mean that the history of the Church from its foundation right up to the present time has necessarily conformed to any pattern in Jesus' mind. It became, inevitably, an institution and so had, at times, to come to terms with the world of men in a way which was alien to his perfectionist outlook. Whenever it associated itself with secular authority, with power politics, and the persecutions of minorities, it deviated in its total aspect from the original teaching of its founder. There was, indeed, as has been pointed out, a certain dualism in the substance of Jesus' spoken word which was a product of his sensitive and uncompromising temperament. He cannot be altogether exonerated from the charge of encouraging the use of violence against the wicked, which in practice came to mean those who did not accept the doctrines of the Church. Such assertions as 'narrow is the gate and straitened the way that leadeth unto life, and few be they that find it' have been in part, albeit indirectly, responsible for an exclusive, even ruthless, attitude towards heretics who, whatever their virtues, from the very fact that they did not 'believe' were regarded as eternally damned. What misery and degradation and suffering have been caused to countless human beings by the practice of such intolerance! We can well understand the poet of scientific humanism writing, *tantum religio potuit suadere malorum*: 'Such were the evils that religion could induce in the minds of men.'

A.I.P.'s reference to the Church as an institution which had 'at times to come to terms with the world of men in a way which was alien to his (Jesus') perfectionist outlook' bids fair to become a classic example of understatement. For it is the fate of all institutions that they should not only 'at times' but all the time wrestle with the problems of achieving some kind of modus vivendi *between what is ideally desirable and what is practically possible.*   W.W.S.

But nothing could be more false, or further from an accurate estimate of Jesus' whole outlook and character, than to suppose that he would have encouraged or condoned any action on the part of his followers that would involve the suffering of human beings. The whole emphasis of his teaching lay in the opposite direction, and he would have looked upon the religious wars and persecutions, the atrocities of Crusade and Inquisition, carried out in his name, with utter and uncomprehending misery. They were a perversion of everything that he had wanted men to be, a hideous distortion of certain expressions he had used in moods of impatience and despair, wantonly torn from the whole context of his life.

With everything in this paragraph I can agree, save one phrase. But that phrase is crucial. It is the reference to Jesus as looking upon religious wars and persecutions 'with utter and uncomprehending misery'. Here, more vividly I think than anywhere else in the book, is summed up the major point of difference between us.

That Jesus would have encouraged or condoned any action that would involve human suffering is, I agree, quite incomprehensible. But that he recognized the inevitability of such action in human affairs is, I believe, certain. If there is one thing that stands out almost more clearly than anything else in the records of his life it is his understanding of human nature. Time and again the writers of the Gospels speak of his 'compassion', his ability to enter into the experience of men and to suffer with them; to take upon himself the consequences of their folly and sin. As the writer of the Fourth Gospel puts it, 'he knew what was in men'.

For that reason, I think, he could never have been a mere spectator of the sins and follies of mankind. Certainly he could never have been an uncomprehending one; least of all could he have looked on with 'utter misery', for that would have meant to concede the victory — which I think he never did. On the contrary, I believe that both the New Testament records and the history of the Church reveal him as an utter and complete realist. He knew that men would not merely fail to achieve the ideal but would even go to the length of trying to destroy it. He knew that in so far as he sought to keep the challenge of the ideal before them he was inviting their opposition.

The truth about the Crucifixion, I believe, is not that defeat and death were forced upon him, but that he virtually forced men into a situation in which they had to choose between denying themselves and all they held most dear or of denying him. That they chose the second, as being in their judgment, however regrettable, the lesser of two evils, came as no surprise to him; and though the acceptance of their verdict involved him in the agony of the Crucifixion, it was not the agony of 'utter misery' but the birth pangs of the new kingdom. For in the last analysis that which prevents most of us from pursuing the ideals that attract us to their logical conclusion is the fear of death – not merely physical death, but the death of the spirit in disillusionment and the apparent loss of things we hold dearer than life itself.

But those who came to see the Cross in the light of the Resurrection were able to see as none had ever seen before that death was not after all the defeat of the ideal but only a stage in the process of its realization.   W.W.S.

When, therefore, we say that Jesus was the main author of Christianity, we are thinking primarily of that broad stream of Christian thought and action which throughout the ages has enriched the experience of mankind and made it possible for the human race to develop its spiritual nature in terms of purity, service and love. It is to this regenerative movement that the founder, drawing on the teaching of the Hebrew prophets, gave the impetus of his own unique personality.

There were, it is true, many by-products of that original inspiration. Religious militancy, in its various forms, we have seen to be one of them. Another was a spiritual withdrawal from life. Jesus taught his disciples to shut the door on themselves when they prayed, and at several moments in his life he withdrew to a secluded spot where he could be alone with his Father. There were also occasional utterances of his which seemed to imply that the wickedness of mankind was such that the individual could only escape contamination by cutting himself free from all the ties of society. This strand of his teaching came to be expressed in all kinds of ascetic practice, and led men in subsequent ages to take monastic vows and a pursue a life of pure contemplation. Yet this is by no means a specifically Christian development. It had

earlier origins, not only among the Essenes but also in the Greek
ascetic schools of thought such as Cynicism, as well as in the
religions of the East. The prime significance of the life and
teaching of Jesus lies in a very different sphere. It is to be found
in the new dynamic he gave to men's social conduct and their
relations to one another. And the effect of this has been felt far
beyond the confines of the Christian Church.

This dynamic had a twofold expression. It gave rise to a new
emphasis on universalism that proclaimed the essential unity and
brotherhood of man without distinction of race or colour or
nationality. And it led men to think in terms of service and sacrifice
for their fellow creatures, to develop a sense of personal responsibility towards what Hamlet so poignantly called 'the heartache
and the thousand natural shocks that flesh is heir to'. Whenever
men in subsequent ages, whether Christian, like St. Francis of
Assisi, or non-Christian, like Mahatma Gandhi, have felt the
intensity of this human urge, they are the spiritual heirs of Jesus of
Nazareth.

The universal outlook, as has been shown, derived originally
from the Hebrew prophets and from such later Old Testament
writings as Ruth and the Book of Jonah. It was proclaimed
unequivocally, too, by the best of the Rabbis, such as the early
Ben Azzai, who thought the verse from Genesis v. 1, 'This is the
book of the generations of *Man*' (Hebrew: 'Adam'), was the most
important in the Bible, since it emphasized the essential unity of the
human race. Jesus, as we have seen, did not altogether shake off
the feelings of national exclusiveness shared by all the Jews of his
time, and which partly derived from a belief in Israel's divine
election. But his emphasis on the individual's responsibility to live
in direct relation with his Maker did, in fact, give a fresh impetus
to the universalistic concept. That is why his followers were able
to formulate a new world-wide religion which transcended all
racial and national barriers, while the older Judaism, for all its
magnificent teaching about universal brotherhood, never quite
succeeded in divesting itself of the trappings of a tribal cult.

This was partly because the Jewish teachers regarded their
monotheistic religion as a sacred trust and feared, not without
some justification, that it would be impoverished and compromised
if it were shared too widely with other peoples who had been
reared in a different and often inferior tradition. Hence the famous

'fence round the Law'. It was the supreme achievement of Jesus that, by insisting on the individual's responsibility in bringing about the kingdom of God, he broke through the barriers of particularism and showed the way by which the concept of universal brotherhood might be brought to fruition. And this was done without any serious breach with traditional Judaism, certainly without any sacrifice of pure monotheistic belief. It is some measure of the significance of that achievement that even today movements for the unification of mankind are based not only on the claims of expediency, but on a spiritual urge derived from Jesus and the Hebrew prophets to bring God's kingdom into the world of men.

The second direct consequence of Jesus' example and teaching has previously been referred to, for want of a better term, as the dynamic of love, stirring in men's hearts and spurring them to action. The Greeks with their fine analytical genius distinguished between several kinds of love, and the word used in the New Testament in regard to Jesus was Agapê. This is neither the love of passion (Eros), nor the love of natural affection (Storgé), but the love that implies service and devotion. In the Old Testament its fullest expression is to be found in the description of the suffering servant of the second Isaiah. This is the picture of a man (or a people) deliberately sacrificing himself for the sins of mankind and vicariously bearing on his shoulders the stripes that men had earned through their wickedness.

This, as we have seen, was the way in which Jesus interpreted his Messianic role, and he took the words of the Prophet quite literally. Such was the intensity of his love and sympathy for his fellow creatures that he was sought out by the sick and sinful, the poor and outcast among them, and he brought them comfort and courage and mental health. When they were ailing in body he used his unique gifts to restore their physical powers; when, through sin or ignorance, they were rejected by society and had come to despise themselves, he gave them new confidence and hope. Many a poor sufferer in that age, belonging to what today we might call the submerged or 'untouchable' classes, owed a new lease of life to the magic of his understanding heart.

And so once again he set a fashion for other men to follow. He showed them that where the usual devices of human society to protect itself against its enemies or misfits – prejudice, ostracism, retribution, forcible restraint – inevitably fail, miracles can be achieved through the chastening power of love. Whenever men have devoted their lives to great human causes such as the abolition of slavery or poverty, whenever they have given up wealth and comfort and distinction in order to work in slums or minister to the poor and ailing, they have been wholly or in part inspired by the example of Jesus. They are still rightly described as 'Christ-like'. Even a Hindu like Gandhi could put up a picture of him on the mud wall of his hut bearing the inscription: 'He is our peace.'

The secret of this magic exerted over all subsequent generations by a young Jew living nearly 2,000 years ago must be found ultimately in that indefinable something which we call personality. It cannot be explained in terms of his teaching, for in a sense he taught nothing new. His theology was the long-established theology of Judaism, and he left behind no new system of philosophy or political thought. The tragedy of his death and the stories of his miraculous survival, though they captured man's imagination, would not in themselves have accounted for the range and depth of his influence. Such martyrdoms were common in ancient times, and the lives of great men are always susceptible to legendary distortion and amplification. He was neither scientist nor artist in the accepted sense of the terms. He was indeed an artist in words and the telling of stories, but this by itself could not have accounted for his perennial fame. His artistry was displayed on the wider canvas of life itself. He came near to showing man how life was to be lived, and the enigma of his achievement is primarily to be explained in terms of the impact of his character on the minds of his contemporaries.

That character was, as in the case of all human beings, compact of strength and weakness. The inevitable contradiction between the aim and performance was more clearly marked than usual, in the case of one who aimed so high; and, like all men of genius, he had the defects of his transcendent qualities. Possessed of that inner harmony of the soul which rests on an unshakable faith in the ultimate goodness of things, he was so baffled by men's worldly conduct that he fell into moods of extreme depression and self-distrust. Certain, beyond most men, of the role he had to play and the rightness of his cause, he showed at times an indecision and fearfulness that could only spring from a lack of confidence in his own powers. A man of exceptional sensitivity, he could be deeply wounded by criticism and personal antagonism. This explained his passionate outbursts, his virulent denunciations and the extreme anguish of his soul.

He cannot be altogether acquitted of the fault he most blamed in others, self-righteousness and spiritual pride. No man who was so certain of the truth, who claimed to have special access to the author of all truth, could fail to show impatience and resentment when his message went unheeded. He could never be detached or dispassionate on issues of right or wrong. He was not the philosopher who was capable of debating the validity of competing moral theories, 'the nicely calculated less or more'. Rather, like the Prophets, he was an unquestioning believer in God's revelation of truth to himself, and so found it impossible to tolerate lesser illuminations. If men were to win salvation, they must give up everything else and follow the way he had shown them; otherwise they were irretrievably lost.

It is doubtful, indeed, whether without this intensity of conviction, this immense concentration of spiritual energy, he could ever have imposed his personality so effectively on his immediate followers and their successors right up to the present time. For they were caught in the fire of his emotional enthusiasm, and their response to the man and his appeal was almost unconscious; they found themselves in the grip of a power they could hardly understand. All they knew was that his presence disturbed them and caused them to do things that they had never dreamed of; and from it somehow they gained that inner peace that passeth all understanding.

For it was not only at the deeper, more austere level that Jesus won their hearts as he has won men's hearts ever since. He must not be thought of as a pure moralist, like Savonarola or John Knox, who conceived it his sole business to stir men's consciences and so shame them into virtue. His supreme gift lay in making virtue attractive. There was grace in all his bearing. If he could alienate those who did not fall under his spell – the complacent, the pedantic, the conventional – to the many who were irresistibly attracted to him, he was the kindly, affectionate, good companion. Children, especially, he loved – 'Of such is the kingdom of heaven'. It is sometimes asked whether he had a sense of humour. No one who studies his brilliant repartees (such as what matters is that which comes out of the mouth rather than that which goes into it), his pungent, chiselled aphorisms or his gentle ironies, can have a doubt about the answer. Intellectually, he had the peculiar rabbinic gift for throwing light on a subject through verbal subtlety, and in argument he often saw two moves ahead of his opponents. His genius was not of the bookish sort but could be expresssd in the ordinary homely language of life, and this enabled him to speak direct to simple, unsophisticated folk, such as the Am-ha-aretz.

In the last analysis, the secret of Jesus' power to change the whole course of history and influence men in countries and ages he had never known lies in this gift for giving and inspiring love. It is through this, rather than any other quality he possessed, that he has captured the world's imagination. Christian doctrine through-out the ages has focused attention on the Crucifixion, and the manner of his death has certainly served for all time as an example to the world's martyrs and those who are willing to sacrifice every-thing for their principles. But to the human race as a whole it is the romantic quality of his life that has proved a permanent incentive. He tried, as few men have tried, to help and cherish and love other human beings and to treat them as brothers, children of their heavenly Father. He did not always succeed – no human being has ever done that. He had, after all, a very short life. Yet it proved long enough for that marked contrast to appear between him and the vast majority of ordinary, decent people; and long enough for the flowering of a genius that caused the whole story of the human race to be differently written.

> That low man seeks a little thing to do,
>   Sees it and does it;
> This high man, with a great thing to pursue,
>   Dies ere he knows it.

There came a point in my re-reading of this chapter at which I felt it to be bordering on impertinence to interrupt any further A.I.P.'s final estimate of Jesus' significance in world history. Now that we have come to the end there is perhaps little that I need add, for I seem already to have commented several times on certain of the points which have recurred in these concluding pages.

Perhaps the crux of the whole matter and of the difference between us is to be seen most clearly in the opening sentences of the paragraph beginning: 'The secret of this magic' [? influence] on page 152. A.I.P.'s conclusion that the ultimate secret is to be found in 'that indefinable something which we call personality' really begs the whole question. But so, I suppose, also does the Christian affirmation that he was 'the Christ, the Son of the Living God'. For while A.I.P. is honest enough to admit that what he calls 'personality' is ultimately indefinable, I fear that we Christians sometimes use the term 'Son of God' as if we knew exactly what it means, instead of acknowledging, as in all conscience we should, that we too are using a term that in the last resort is indefinable.

And yet I cannot help feeling that although neither of us may have the complete and final solution of the mystery, the faith which affirms that in Jesus we have not merely man's nearest approach to God, but also God's nearest approach to man – even to the extent of becoming incarnate in man – comes nearer to the heart of the ultimate mystery than any attempt, however sincerely and genuinely conceived, to explain the profound and lasting impression of Jesus on all subsequent history in terms simply of 'personality'.

But it was no part of the purpose of our collaboration in this book that either should attempt to prove the other right or wrong in any particular, though we agreed at the outset that it was not only desirable but necessary that major points of difference between us should be frankly and, so far as considerations of space would allow, fully stated.

In two things, however, we are agreed. The first is the recognition that whatever may be the doctrinal differences between Christians and Jews, and indeed between Christians and men of all other faiths or of none, in respect of their attitude to the historical person of Jesus of Nazareth, the importance of his contribution to human history is such that he cannot be ignored. In these circumstances it is reasonable to assume – as indeed it has been the whole purpose of this book to demonstrate – that as in the case of all other of the great personages of history, a better knowledge of the historical, religious and domestic background of his life and work is essential to any understanding of the person himself.

Our second point of fundamental agreement is this: that however much we may differ in our interpretation of his person, it is impossible to ignore the challenge of his teaching. It is my own personal view – and here I would stress that I am in no way committing my colleague – that it is only as we give serious consideration to that challenge that we can hope ever to come to grips with the mystery of his person. W.W.S.

INDEX

Aaron, 31, 35, 45
Acts of the Apostles, 68
Akibah (Rabbi), 97
Albigenses, 52
Alexander the Great, 18, 21 ff., 37
Alexandria, 23, 37, 47, 143
Am-ha-aretz, 49, 56 f., 74, 81, 84, 87, 154
Amoraim, 70
Amos, 14, 32, 38, 74
Ananias, 70
Andrew, 80
Antiochus Epiphanes, 23 ff., 47
Antipater, 27
Apocalypse, 38 ff., 140; apocalyptic literature, 38 ff.; prophecies, 38, 79, 97; Pharisees, 50, 77, 110, 131
Apocrypha, 24, 37, 118
Archelaus, 27, 60, 91
Aretas IV, 77
Ark of the Covenant, 12
Ashtoreth, 31
Asshurbanipal, 36
Assyria, 12, 14 f., 20 f., 33

Baalim, 31
Babylon, 10, 15 ff., 20, 22, 36, 46
Barabbas, 103
Bar Mitzvah, 76
Beatitudes, 118 f.
Ben Azzai (Rabbi), 150
Ben Sira, 37
Berith Milah (Circumcision), 73
Bethany, 93, 95, 98
Beth Din (Court of Law), 48, 62; see also Sanhedrin
Bethlehem, 140
Bethphage, 92

Caesarea, 60 f., 68, 83, 89
Caiaphas, 101 f.
Capernaum, 81, 84, 91
Chassidim, 47, 82

Christianity, 22, 139; doctrines, 65, 129, 137, 141 f., 145; Jesus as founder of, 66, 146 f., 149; the early Church, 53, 63, 65 f.; later development, 31, 147 ff.; humanitarian role, 149 f.
Cleomenes III, 143
Corban, 87, 130
Crucifixion, 65, 104 ff., 108 f., 126, 137, 149 ff., 154; responsibility for, 103, 108 f.
Cynicism, 150
Cyrus, 16 f., 33, 38

Damascus, 19, 65, 74
Daniel, 17, 38 f., 79
David, 13, 19, 22, 37 f.; see also Messiah
Day of Judgment, 38, 40, 79, 112
Dead Sea Scrolls, 52 f.
Decapolis, 89, 91
Delphi, 12, 16
Deutero-Isaiah, 16, 33 f., 151
Deuteronomic Reformation, 14 ff., 32, 106

Ecclesiastes, 23, 37
Edom, 10, 25 ff.
Egypt, 21 f., 24, 33, 73
Eliezer the Great (Rabbi), 71
Elijah, 14, 77 f., 90, 140
Elohim, 31
Enoch (Book of), 37 ff.
Essenes, 10, 52 f., 56, 58, 77, 86, 93, 121, 131, 150
Ezekiel, 16, 22, 32 f., 39, 46
Ezra, 20, 22, 23, 34 f., 46

Fourth Philosophy, 53

Galilee, 10, 25, 26, 53, 56, 58 f., 73 f., 79 ff., 88 ff., 100, 102 f., 118, 137, 141, 147